Latch On to Literature

A Teacher's Guide
to 12 Caldecott Medal
and Honor Books

by Jody Hamm

Alleyside
Press

Cover art by Pat Topper

Published by Alleyside Press, a Division of Freline, Inc.
P. O. Box 889
Hagerstown, MD 21741

ISBN 0-913853-27-5

Printed in the United States of America

Contents

Introduction

This collection of Caldecott Award and Honor books represents a wide variety of types of illustrations as well as a wide variety of stories. Each book contains the following information:

- Reading level of the book
- Interest level of the book
- Brief biography of the author and/or illustrator
- Synopsis
- Theme or central thought of the story
- Literary objectives
- Discussion questions (two to six lessons)
- Concluding critical thinking exercises
- Concluding extension activities
- Additional readings

Many Caldecott Award and Honor books are derived from folktales and for this reason, several are included in this collection. Most folktales tend to be multileveled and therefore make excellent sources for teaching and reviewing some of the literary expressions for older children as well as younger ones.

The following can be used as a general outline to discuss illustrations with older children:

1. Define the term *artist's style.* Concepts should include the way the illustrator interprets the story.

2. Questions that can be used toward analyzing the illustrations include:

   a. What does the picture tell you about the content?
   b. How much of the story can you imagine by looking at the picture?
   c. What does the artist use to get you to imagine?
   d. Does the artist's style fit the story? Why or why not?

The above questions should help children pay more attention to the illustrations and be able to make judgements about the contribution of illustrations to understanding and appreciating the story.

3. Because folktales are generally multileveled, they can be interpreted at a level appropriate to the reader.

With young children, some of the concluding questions and activities will be too difficult for one student to do alone, but could be used with the whole class or group. These activities should get the students in the habit of reading critically and therefore thinking out their answers instead of giving general "yes–no" answers. Critical reading is a difficult skill to develop, but by beginning early with discussion in a non-threatening atmosphere, students should be able to develop higher levels of thinking. By the time they are older, it will be a natural process.

The lesson divisions are purely subjective. These can—and should—be changed according to the individual abilities and maturity of each particular group of students.

The concluding critical thinking exercises and extensions are also merely guidelines and suggestions. Students certainly should not be expected to do all of them, particularly if they are working individually. It is our intention to facilitate the *love* of reading, not the *hate* of it!

Listed below are general behavioral objectives for this book. However, every adult working with children in reading should keep foremost in mind that the goal is to develop the love of reading in students, who will develop their skills to become lifetime readers— not only when forced to for information, but for enjoyment as well.

1. Students will develop an awareness and appreciation of a wide variety of illustrations.

2. Students will develop an awareness and appreciation of a wide variety of good literature.

3. Students will develop and increase their oral and written communication skills.

4. Students will develop and increase their vocabulary skills.

5. Students will develop and make use of higher level critical thinking skills including analysis, synthesis, and evaluation.

My objective from the onset of this project has been to assist the already overworked classroom teacher and librarian.

When using literature as the basis for teaching reading, care must be taken not to lose sight of basic skills that you are responsible for teaching.

Discussion questions for each guide are generally literal comprehension questions. Answers have been provided for these discussion questions when available. Generally, when the answers may vary, the questions are from a higher level of questioning.

I fully believe reading can be taught and made more exciting using nothing except good literature books. However, in this day and age of accountability, you, as a teacher, need to be thoroughly knowledgeable of your school's course of study. This will keep you attuned with the basic skills you are responsible for teaching.

At the end of the book, I have included some forms that can be duplicated and used for story development, character development, and comprehension development.

Happy reading!

Alexander and the Wind-Up Mouse

by Leo Lionni

New York: Pantheon, 1969

Reading Level: 2   **Interest Level: K–3**

Author

Leo Lionni was born May 5, 1910, in Amsterdam, Holland. He came to the United States in 1939 and became a naturalized citizen in 1945. He attended schools in Holland, Belgium, the United States, Italy, and Switzerland, and received his Ph.D. at the University of Genoa.

Lionni has been a freelance writer, art director for N. W. Ayer & Son, Inc. (advertising firm), an illustrator of children's books, and the head of the graphic design department at the Parsons School of Design, among other things. He has also had many one-man shows of his paintings, and sculpture in galleries and museums in the U.S. and Europe.

About his writings, Lionni claims he is not conscious of the average age of his potential readers. He "believes that a good children's book should appeal to all people who have not completely lost their original joy and wonder in life."

Synopsis

A real mouse and a mechanical mouse become friends. Problems arise when the mechanical toy is thrown away. With the help of a magic lizard, the mechanical toy is turned into a real mouse.

Theme or Central Thought

1. The grass is always greener. . . .

2. Development of friendships.

3. Growing up.

Literary Objectives

1. The student will be able to describe the main parts of the story—plot (what happens), characters (who does it happen to), and setting (where it happens).

2. The student will be able to compare the characteristics of a real mouse with the characteristics of Alex.

3. The student will be able to identify the theme, or the main idea, of the story.

4. The student will be able to compare storytelling and fables.

DISCUSSION QUESTIONS

Lesson 1

Before reading the book, leaf through and discuss the illustrations in the book and how they differ from illustrations in other books.

In the first lesson with this book, you might want to start by reading the story aloud to the students. After completion, discuss the illustrations and the vocabulary as presented in the lessons that follow.

Lesson 2

Vocabulary words you might want to discuss before reading:

directions	crumbs	chase	broom
squawk	ordinary	around	circles
cuddle	between	kitchen	everybody
adventures	mousetraps	penguin	whispered
mysteriously	pebblepath	suddenly	

1. On the first page, why did Alexander run for his hole as fast as possible? *(Cups, saucers, and spoons were flying in all directions.)*

2. Why do you think these things were flying in all directions? *(Answers will vary; actually, Alexander wanted a few crumbs.)*

3. How did Alexander find the other mouse? *(No one was in the house and he heard a squeak.)*

4. How was this other mouse different? *(It had wheels instead of legs and on its back was a key.)*

5. What was the first thing Willy explained about himself? *(He said he was Annie's favorite toy.)* Do you think it was important that he began with this? *(Answers will vary.)*

6. How did Willy sleep? *(On a soft white pillow between the doll and a woolly teddy bear.)*

7. What do you think is the reason for the picture with the boots? Explain this illustration. *(The story does not mention the boots.)*

8. Why did Alexander want to be like Willy? *(To be cuddled and loved.)*

9. Do you think Alexander was jealous of Willy? *(Answers will vary.)*

10. Why did Willy tell Alexander about the magic lizard? *(Answers will vary.)*

Lesson 3

Vocabulary words you may want to discuss before reading:

quivering	in vain	pantry	surprised
hugged	excited	precious	rustled
blinding	alas	baseboard	cautiously
frightened			

1. What did the magic lizard tell Alexander he had to do? *(He had to bring the lizard a purple pebble when the moon is round.)*

2. Was it easy for Alexander to find the purple pebble? *(No. He found every other color, but no purple.)*

3. What did he discover when he returned to the house? *(Willy was going to be thrown away.)*

4. Where do you think he found the purple pebble? *(Answers will vary.)*

5. Why do you think Alexander changed his mind about the wish he wanted? *(Answers will vary.)*

6. Why is the picture dark when Alexander is running back to the house? *(Answers may vary, but if the moon is round, it is probably night.)*

7. What does it mean when the story says: ". . . with a heavy heart he went to his hole . . ."? *(He was very sad.)*

8. Why do you think Alexander moved cautiously toward the hole? *(He was afraid.)*

9. Did he recognize Willy? How do we know? *(No, or Willy would not have had to introduce himself.)*

CONCLUDING CRITICAL THINKING EXERCISES

1. What makes some toys more valuable or more likely to be favorites than others?

2. When you have to clean out your toy box and discard some of the toys, how do you choose which ones to throw away?

3. When do you most need your favorite stuffed animal or toy? Why?

4. How do you think Annie felt about having another mouse in the house? Or do you think she knew about the other mouse?

5. What do you think happened after the last page? Write a new ending.

6. Why do you think many children sleep with toys or stuffed animals? Did you know that Prince Charles and Princess Diana of England still sleep with stuffed animals as adults? (The Prince still has his favorite teddy bear, which has been mended many times.)

7. At the end of the story, Alexander was afraid to go back to his hole in the baseboard. What makes people afraid of doing things?

8. This story could be written as a fable. What would be the moral if it were a fable? Compare this story with another having the same moral.

CONCLUDING EXTENSION ACTIVITIES

Suggestions follow for specific as well as general activities that can be used with this book. A complete list of general activities can be found at the end of the book.

1. Make an original collage for *Alexander and the Wind-Up Mouse* using any kind of media available. The collage should tie in to the story. Look at the illustrations in the book. How are they different? How does the illustrator change the moods of the characters? Working in pairs, try to do it with some scraps of paper.

2. Write a couplet that could be used by Alexander when he is looking for the magic lizard.

3. Skim through the book and write as many color words as you can find. With your crayons, write the color of each word. You might want to put these in a booklet in the shape of a mouse.

4. Cut out pictures of toys you'd like to have from a catalog. Write a reason for each of your choices.

5. Create an original character or toy and tell how it would fit into *Alexander and the Wind-Up Mouse.*

6. Rewrite the story in the form of a play or puppet show.

7. Make puppets of the characters for the show by cutting out wallpaper and gluing to the end of a straw.

8. Fold a large piece of paper into eight sections. Draw a different part of the story in each section, then retell the story in your own words to another group who has not read or heard the story.

9. Make a cassette tape, reading the story so that other children can follow along. You will want to put some kind of a noise to indicate it's time to turn the page.

ADDITIONAL WRITINGS BY LEO LIONNI

It's Mine. New York: Pantheon, 1986.

Let's Make Rabbits: A Fable. New York: Pantheon, 1982.

Nicolas, Where Have You Been? New York: Pantheon, 1987.

Six Crows. New York: Pantheon, 1988.

Duffy and the Devil

Retold by Harve Zemach

Illustrated by Margot Zemach

New York, Farrar: Straus, and Giroux, 1973

Reading Level: 4   Interest Level: 2–5

Author

Harve Zemach was born December 5, 1933, in Newark, New Jersey. He married illustrator Margot Zemach January 29, 1957. Their children are Kaethe, Heidi, and Rachel. He received his B.A. in 1955 from Wesleyan University at Middletown, Connecticut. He did graduate studies at the University of Vienna and received his M.A. in 1959 from Brandeis University.

Besides being an author of juvenile books, Zemach has also been an instructor in history and social science at Boston University.

Illustrator

Illustrator Margot Zemach was born on November 30, 1931, in Los Angeles, California. She married author Harve Zemach January 29, 1957. She attended several art institutes and studied at Vienna Academy of Fine Arts under a Fulbright scholarship in 1955–56.

She received the Caldecott Award in 1974 for the illustrations in this book. She also received a Caldecott Honor award in 1970 for *The Judge: An Untrue Tale,* and a Caldecott Honor award in 1978 for *It Could Always Be Worse: A Yiddish Folktale.*

Ms. Zemach has very definite opinions about the illustrations in children's books. She says, "The modern trend of oversimplification is impossible; it's merely foisting designers' ideas on children." She claims, "Children are fascinated by detail." An example she cites is "Take a child to the zoo and you may well find that amid all the exotic beasts, it's the pigeon walking around the child's feet that catches his attention."

Synopsis

(Quotes from the book jacket.) A Cornish version of the old Rumpelstiltskin folktale, this book was the 1974 Caldecott Medal Book. It "was originally a popular play in Cornwall in the nineteenth century, performed at the Christmas season by groups of young people who went from house to house. . . ."

"The language spoken by the Christmas players was a rich mixture of local English dialect and Old Cornish (similar to Welsh and Gaelic), and something of this flavor is preserved in Harve Zemach's retelling. . . ."

This is a Cornish tale retold in which a devil agrees to help Duffy, a lazy and clumsy hired girl, do her spinning and knitting for three years, but all will be taken away unless Duffy is able to tell the devil his name. The old housekeeper helps Duffy by luring the Squire to the devil's hideaway.

The illustrations in this Caldecott award book help portray and interpret the characters.

Theme or Central Thought

1. There is danger in falsifying self-accomplishments.

2. Lying is usually detected.

3. Deception is dishonest.

Literary Objectives

1. The student will be able to develop an appreciation of folklore.

2. When given another book of folklore, the student will be able to identify it as folklore.

3. The student will be able to develop the ability to analyze folklore and compare the same theme in differing countries.

DISCUSSION QUESTIONS

Lesson 1

1. From the title and the front of the book, can you predict what kind of story this is going to be? *(Answers will vary. Lead the group to the idea that this is a folktale and very probably not true. Try to get them to see the little character behind the tree and to guess that he is the devil.)*

2. Skim through the book and tell how many main characters you think are in the story. *(Answers will vary. There are only the man and his housekeeper [children will guess this to be his wife, but it isn't], Duffy [who has the pigtails], and the devil.)*

3. Can you predict which character you think is Duffy? *(Answers will vary.)*

4. Look at the pictures at the end of the book. Can you predict what has happened? *(Answers will vary.)*

Lesson 2

Point out that *Duffy and the Devil* is an old Cornish tale and contains many words that we do not use, but that their meanings will be discussed later.

Read the first two pages aloud and then ask:

1. What do you think a squire is? *(Answers will vary, but lead children to understand that it is an English title of dignity given to certain gentlemen.)*

2. On the first page, where is Squire Lovel going? *(He is going to Buryan Churchtown to find a helper for his housekeeper.)*

3. Why does his housekeeper need a helper? *(She is getting old and cannot see to do things such as spinning, sewing, and knitting.)*

4. What is the old woman angry about? *(She claims Duffy pays too much attention to the boys and doesn't get her work done.)*

5. Is Duffy who you think she was? *(Go back to the predictions from the pictures.)*

6. Do you think Duffy is telling the truth? Why? *(Answers will vary. Invite several of the students to tell you why they believe as they do.)*

Vocabulary words that may need to be discussed after the first two pages (emphasize throughout that it is not always necessary to know the exact meanings of words; often, the meaning can be found through the context of the sentence):

squire	screeching	bufflehead	confloption
gashly	gallivants	clouts	clumps

Read as far as the picture with the furniture and everything all askew. After reading, ask the following:

1. Do you want to change your prediction of Duffy? Why? *(Most will probably want to change at this point.)*

2. The first part of this reading says that Duffy "sat herself ladylike behind him." From the picture, do you think she is sitting "ladylike"? *(Answers will vary.)*

3. Why is his house called "Trove Manor"? *(Answers will vary. Trove is the name of the large farm area and manor means it's the main house at this estate.)*

4. The last sentence states: "The devil can make Squire Lovel's stockings for all I care!" Can you predict what is going to happen? Why? *(Answers will vary, but make certain students can defend their answers. They should be encouraged to make predictions, but their predictions must make sense to the story.)*

After this reading, discuss the many expressions in this book, such as:

"Good riddance to bad rummage!"

"sat herself ladylike behind him"

"Duffy ate her fill"

"Curse the spinning!"

"The devil can make Squire Lovel's stockings for all I care"

Continue reading the next five pages, ending with the scene outside the church. After reading this section, ask the following:

17

1. We finally meet up with the devil. How fast could he spin? See if you can find the words that tell this. *(". . . his fingers flying so fast that Duffy couldn't even see them . . .")*

2. What features make the devil look like a real person? *(Possible answers: hands, feet and legs, beard, eyes, nose, mouth.)*

3. What things make him look unreal? *(Tail and horns.)*

4. What did the devil make first? *(He knitted a pair of stockings.)*

5. What kind of deal did the devil make with Duffy? *(He told her he would do all her knitting and spinning, but at the end of three years he would take it all away unless she could tell him his name.)*

6. Did the squire like his new stockings? *(Yes.)*

7. Where did the squire wear his new stockings? *(Hunting and to church.)*

8. Would you wear the same pair of stockings to these two places? *(Answers will vary. Most students will say no, but point out that these were "soft as silk" and "strong as leather.")*

9. Where is everyone in the illustration with all the people standing around talking? *(Probably in front of the church.)*

   After the scene outside the church, discuss the following:

   "oogly little squinny-eyed creature"

   "whillygogs and whizamagees"

   "Simple as pudding"

   "fingers flying"

   "couple of blinks"

   "without your lifting a finger"

   "trudging through furze and brambles"

   "plodging through brake and briar"

Lesson 3

Continue reading the next four pages. After reading, ask the following questions:

1. What did the squire ask Duffy to make? *(A new hunting jacket.)*

2. Do you think Duffy is worried about the deal with the devil? Try to find the words that answer this question. *(No; "she just put it out of mind.")*

3. Before reading the next page, ask: What do you think is happening in the next two pictures? *(Answers will vary. The children may guess that the person with the squire is Duffy, but will probably think it is some kind of party.)*

4. (After reading:) Is there anything in these pictures that might suggest that the squire married Duffy? *(Answers will vary. Point out there is no church, no wedding ring, no bridal gown, and that you would have to read to really know the answer to this. Try to conclude that the pictures don't always tell the whole story.)*

After the pages, discuss:

> "shrugged her shoulders and did her deal"
> "on the green by the mill"

Continue reading the next two pages. After reading, ask the following:

1. Is Duffy beginning to get worried about her deal with the devil? Find the words that tell the answer. *(Yes. "That set her grieving over her troubles.")*

2. Why do you think Duffy told Jone her troubles? *(Answers will vary.)*

3. Do you find anything strange in the picture on the right? *(Jone is smoking a pipe.)*

4. Make predictions as to what you think will happen.

After these pages, discuss:

> "jibing and jeering"
> "behaving all cock-a-hoop"
> "cellar"

Continue reading the next six pages, ending with the picture of the witches chasing the squire. Ask the following:

1. Why didn't the squire go home? *(He hated to go home empty-handed and he had found a hare.)*

2. Do you think the witches work for the devil? *(Answers will vary.)*

3. Do you think that is really Jone playing the fiddle? *(Answers will vary. Point out the sentence about the beer and remind the children what Jone told Duffy.)*

4. Why do you think the witches are chasing him? *(Answers will vary.)*

Continue reading the next four pages, ending with "they went to bed." Then ask the following:

1. Do you think the squire has made any connection between Duffy and what happened that evening? *(No.)*

2. Why did the squire laugh and laugh? *(Duffy was laughing so much that it made him laugh.)*

3. Can you predict how the story is going to end? *(Answers will vary.)*

Continue reading to the end of the story. Then ask the following:

1. How do you think the devil realized Duffy didn't guess, but was told? *(Answers will vary. Point out, however, that Duffy made no hesitation when she said his name.)*

2. Why is the squire pictured with no clothes on? *(The devil turned all his knitting to ashes.)*

3. Why was Jone "sweeping up little piles of ashes"? *(All of the squire's things that had been made by the devil were turned to ashes.)*

4. Did the story end the way you thought it would? *(Answers will vary.)*

5. Do you think Jone will stay with Duffy and Squire Lovel? *(Answers will vary.)*

After the end of the story, discuss:

"he tramped over the moors"

"fuggy-hole"

"ragwort"

"Astride giant leeks"

"gawk-eyed"

"folic"

"goggly"

CONCLUDING CRITICAL THINKING EXERCISES

1. The book was divided up into eight segments when reading aloud. Brainstorm and think up titles for each of the eight segments, each representing the main idea for the segment.

2. Diagram or categorize parts of the story that were funniest, saddest, happiest, and most believable.

3. *Duffy and the Devil* is a form of the story of *Rumpelstiltskin*. Read a version of this story (for example, the 1987 honor book *Rumpelstiltskin* illustrated by Paul O. Zelinsky) and compare and contrast the two. The Compare and Contrast chart can be reproduced for this activity.

4. Compare the illustrations in the above two mentioned books. Discuss why they were selected as Caldecott books.

5. If the story of *Duffy and the Devil* were to have a lesson like fables do, what could the lesson be? Think of one that would be appropriate and be able to defend why you thought of it.

6. Write an original story with the same story plot as the one used in *Duffy and the Devil*.

7. This story was told by the author as the narrator. We call this the *point of view*. What if this story was told from the devil's point of view? How would it be different? With a group of children, rewrite the story from the devil's point of view.

8. Pretend you have to defend this book and you have to convince a group of parents to buy it for their children for a present.

9. Pretend your mother and father are famous actors. They are asked to star in a movie based on this book to portray Duffy and Squire Lovel. They really don't want to do this, as they have planned a big vacation. You have to convince them to be in this movie.

CONCLUDING EXTENSION ACTIVITIES

Suggestions for specific as well as general activities that can be used with this book follow. A complete list of general activities can be found at the end of the book.

1. Make a "WANTED" poster for the devil.

2. Make a time line of the events in the life of Duffy.

3. Reproduce the Story Mapping outline on large chart paper. (If the students are advanced enough, give each a small copy to fill out at the same time.)

4. Make a chart or poster so that others will want to read this book. Make it as colorful as possible.

5. Design a bulletin board about this book. (A project for older children could be to use an opaque projector and reproduce the illustrations from the book.)

6. Make finger puppets of all the characters and then act out the story.

7. Design a new original book cover for the book.

8. Make one or more bookmarks for this book using the characters portrayed in the story.

9. Make paper dolls of all the characters. Be sure to make the different dress changes for Duffy and Squire Lovel.

10. Create an original character or animal and tell how it would fit into the story.

ADDITIONAL READINGS WITH THE SAME THEME

Belpré, Pure. *Oté: A Puerto Rican Folktale.* Illustrated by Paul Galdone, New York: Pantheon, 1969.

Zelinsky, Paul O. *Rumpelstiltskin.* Retold and illustrated by Paul O. Zelinsky, New York: Dutton, 1986.

Frog and Toad Are Friends

by Arnold Lobel

New York: Harper & Row, 1970

Reading Level: 2   Interest Level: K–3

Author

Arnold Lobel was born May 22, 1933, in Los Angeles, California, and died in 1987 in New York, N.Y. He was married to Anita Kempler, who was also a writer and illustrator of children's books. They had two children, Adrianne and Adam. Lobel was a very prolific writer and illustrator of children's books and was awarded several honors for his work.

Arnold Lobel decided early in his life that he would pursue an art career. He entered Pratt Institute, where he discovered that his specialty was book illustration. While there he met his future wife, Anita Kempler, who was also a student at Pratt. They married following graduation in 1955. He began his art career in advertising but was illustrating books by the late 1950s. In the beginning, he had no intention of also becoming a writer.

Synopsis

This book contains five unrelated stories personified by Toad and Frog. Children can relate to the theme of each story and except for the fact that they are personified, their themes could happen to real children. The very fact that they are personified by Toad and Frog might better allow children to see themselves and their friends.

Theme or Central Thought

1. Consideration and trust in friendships.

2. Relationships between friends.

3. Use of animals to portray human qualities.

Literary Objectives

1. The student will be able to understand and to recognize the main parts of a story—plot (what happens), characters (who it happens to), and setting (where it happens).

2. The student will be able to compare and contrast a frog with a toad.

3. The student will be able to recognize the use of personification (giving human qualities to animals).

DISCUSSION QUESTIONS

Lesson 1

You might first want to discuss some of the characteristics and the differences between frogs and toads before beginning this story. Below are some items to help you get started:

1. Frogs are generally slim and speedy.

2. A frog's skin is usually smooth; toads have warts.

3. Most frogs live in or near water; adult toads can live in drier places.

4. Both frogs and toads lay eggs in water—frogs in clumps; toads in strings of double strands.

5. True toads can range in size from 1" to 9" and are mostly nocturnal.

6. Most toads have ridges on top of their heads.

7. Toads have a swelling behind their eyes, which is a defense mechanism.

8. Contrary to myth, toads do not cause warts in humans and are not poisonous to touch.

9. After mating, toads may move far from water. Toads have a tough skin that reduces loss of water.

10. Toads eat plants as tadpoles; they eat insects as adults.

11. Toads should be valued in gardens for pest control.

12. Frogs are also mostly nocturnal.

13. Most frogs have a pair of folds that run down their backs. (Bullfrogs lack these.)

14. Frogs are becoming less common because of widespread pollution and destruction of wetland habitat.

15. Frogs can be green or brown.

16. Frogs cannot adapt to land as toads can.

Lesson 2

Story 1: "Spring"

Vocabulary:

Spring	shelters	tore (tear)	November
blinked	answer	knocked	through
calendar	Blah	meadow	

1. Who is knocking at the front door? *(Frog.)*

2. Why didn't Toad answer the door? *(He wanted to sleep some more.)*

3. When did Toad want to be awakened? *(Half past May.)* What do you think this means? *(Answers may vary.)*

4. How did Frog trick Toad? *(He tore several months off the calendar to make Toad think it was May.)*

5. Was Toad convinced it was May? *(Yes.)* Why do you think he was so trusting of Frog? *(Answers may vary but could include the fact that they are friends.)*

6. Can you think of a time when you were tricked in a similar method? *(Answers will vary.)*

Lesson 3

Story 2: "The Story"

Vocabulary:

quite	thought	perhaps	porch
poured	could	against	terrible
would			

Before reading, ask: In the picture on page 17, tell what you think is happening. *(Answers will vary.)*

1. In whose house are Frog and Toad? *(Toad's house.)*

2. What does Toad give Frog? *(A cup of hot tea.)*

3. Do you have something special that you eat or drink when you're sick? *(Answers will vary.)*

4. What were some of the things Toad did to try to think of a story? *(Walked up and down on the porch; stood on his head; poured water over his head; banged his head against the wall.)*

5. What happened to Toad? *(He got sick.)*

6. Explain the turn of events. *(Frog told Toad the story of what just happened.)*

Lesson 4

Story 3: "A Lost Button"

Vocabulary:

drat	beautiful	sparrow	raccoon
wailed	square	screamed	shelf
sewed			

1. Where did Frog and Toad go first to look for the button? *(Large meadow.)*

2. Who else helped Frog and Toad hunt for the button? *(Sparrow and raccoon.)*

3. Describe, in order, the buttons found. *(Black one, one with two holes, small one, square one, thin one.)*

4. Where did they find the thin button? *(In the mud at the river.)*

5. Why did Toad give his jacket to Frog? *(Guilt for putting Frog through a lot of trouble.)*

6. Do you think Frog understood why Toad gave him the jacket? *(Answers will vary.)*

Lesson 5

Story 4: "A Swim"

Vocabulary:

splashes	lizards	crawled	dragonflies
shiver	sneeze	laugh	

1. Why did Toad not want anyone to look at him in his bathing suit? *(Toad thought he looked funny in it.)*

2. Have you ever tried to cover up something you thought looked funny on you, such as a new haircut? *(Answers will vary.)*

3. Why did Toad finally come out of the water, even though so many were watching? *(He was getting cold and starting to shiver and sneeze.)*

4. Describe Toad's attitude as he was walking away. *(Answers will vary but could include more confident.)*

Lesson 6

Story 5: "The Letter"

Vocabulary:

matter	hurried	envelope	sure
tired	ever	pleased	

1. Why was Toad looking very sad? *(It was time for the mail and he never got any.)*

2. Why do you think Frog sat and looked sad also? *(Answers may vary but possibly to keep Toad company in his sadness.)*

3. After Frog wrote a letter to Toad, do you think he made a wise choice by giving the letter to a snail for delivery? *(Answers will vary. Discuss the pace at which a snail moves.)*

4. Do you think Frog realized the letter would not arrive that day? Give a reason for your answer. *(Probably not, or he would not have gone to Toad's house right away.)*

5. Why did Frog write Toad a letter? *(Because they were best friends.)*

6. How long did it take the snail to deliver the letter? *(Four days.)*

CONCLUDING CRITICAL THINKING EXERCISES

1. In the illustrations of this book, Arnold Lobel used shades of green and brown. Why do you think he chose these colors? Do you think it was a good choice?

2. Give at least five reasons why you think this book was chosen as a Caldecott Honor Book.

3. With the class or a small group, brainstorm ideas about this book and why parents should buy it for their children. Be specific with your reasons.

4. Write an additional chapter that tells a story about you and your best friend.

5. List several ways Frog and Toad showed their friendship.

6. Select which character, Frog or Toad, you would most like to spend a day with and state your reasons.

7. Create an original character or animal and tell how it would fit into the story.

CONCLUDING EXTENSION ACTIVITIES

Suggestions for specific as well as general activities that can be used with this book follow. A complete list of general activities can be found at the end of the book.

1. Make finger puppets of Frog and Toad plus the other animal characters in this book and then act out the different parts of the book.

2. Research the differences between real toads and real frogs. Make a comparison chart for these differences.

3. Each chapter has a vocabulary list. Put each word on a frog, button, mailbox, or something symbolic of this book. Then put all the words together and rank them in ABC order.

4. Design a bulletin board about this book. Make large pictures for your bulletin board.

5. Create a colorful mural on the chalkboard or on a long piece of paper telling each of the parts of the story.

6. Make one or more bookmarks for this book using characters or some event in the story.

7. Make a cassette tape, reading the story so that other children can follow along. (Be sure to put a noise of some kind to indicate to the listener to turn the page.)

8. Make a diorama of one of the scenes of the story.

9. Write a letter to Toad telling what you like about him.

OTHER BOOKS BY ARNOLD LOBEL

Days with Frog and Toad.

Frog and Toad All Year.

Frog and Toad Together.

Goldilocks and the Three Bears

Retold and illustrated by

James Marshall

New York: Dial Books for Young Readers, 1988

Reading Level: 2   Interest Level: 2–4

Background Information

According to the *Oxford Companion to Children's Literature* (Carpenter & Pritchard), *The Three Bears* was first printed in 1837 in a book of essays titled *The Doctor* by Robert Southey. "The narrator introduces the tale as one that was told to the doctor by his uncle William. . . ." The biggest change through the years has been the evolution of Goldilocks. In the original printing, this character was a little old woman who said bad words. She is referred to as "the naughty old Woman." In subsequent renditions, the intruder takes the form of a fox and then, a little girl named Silver-Hair, Silver-Locks, and Golden Hair. "The first use of the name Goldilocks . . . seems to have been in *Old Nursery Stories and Rhymes* illustrated by John Hassall (c. 1904)." Also in some disagreement is the ending of the story: "Some modern versions conclude with Goldilocks running off into the world, while others finish with her coming home, telling her mother what happened, and promising to be a good girl in the future."

Author

James Marshall was born on October 10, 1942, in San Antonio, Texas. He attended New England Conservatory of Music in Boston, Trinity College, and received his B.A. in 1967 from Southern Connecticut State College. He is completely self-taught in art, having attended no art schools. He started his career as a French and Spanish teacher, but has been a freelance writer and illustrator since 1970.

Marshall has mostly stopped illustrating works by other authors, preferring to work on his own texts. He designs all of his books.

He is an admirer of Ludwig Bemelmans' "Madeline" books and admits he has often been inspired by Maurice Sendak. He also deeply admires the work of Arnold Lobel.

Synopsis

James Marshall gives a new twist to this old folktale. In his retelling, Goldilocks is no longer the sweet, innocent little girl who happens to find a house in the woods. She deliberately disobeys her mother, takes the shortcut through the forest, and finds the bears' house. She walks in without knocking and proceeds to try the porridge, chairs, and beds. Marshall updates the illustrations and vocabulary, certainly making this folktale more meaningful to the modern child.

Theme or Central Thought

1. Use of animals to portray human qualities.

2. Appreciation of folktales.

Literary Objectives

1. The student will be able to develop an awareness and appreciation of different styles of the same story.

2. The student will be able to develop the ability to critique and analyze author's style (way of writing, including word choices; sentence structure; repetition; figurative language.)

DISCUSSION QUESTIONS

Lesson 1

Before actually studying this book as literature, read one of the more traditional forms of this title (for example, *The Three Bears* by Paul Galdone). Then read this version to the students with expression. See if they pick up on the repetition of "I don't mind if I do." Also emphasize expressions that might be more associated with modern times.

Discuss the Victorian era and things that might be associated with that time period as well as expressions and manner of dress. Discuss why this period is referred to by this name.

Vocabulary words and expressions that you might want to discuss before reading:

neighbor	muffins	naughty	exactly
meanwhile	clearing	Patooie	scalding
inviting	coarse	comfortable	tuckered
scarcely	parlor	smithereens	amused
Egads	popped	proper	explanation

1. On the cover, what kind of bicycle is the bear family riding? *(Bicycle built for two, or tandem.)*

2. Skim through all the illustrations and find things that might be more likely found in the home of someone older or of someone living in an older time. *(Answers may vary, but could include: bicycle built for two, telephone on the wall, latticework under house, hat of mama bear, glasses on Mama and Papa, lots of sunflowers, dishes displayed on cupboard, puffy chairs with ornate trim, fancy throw on mantel, flowered run, sign "Bless Our Happy Home," oil lamp, canopy bed, old-fashioned toys.)*

3. The bear family dresses in what might be considered a Victorian manner and their house looks Victorian also. Do you think Goldilocks also dresses as they did in that time? *(Answers will vary.)*

4. Describe the first picture. Which person thinks Goldilocks is a sweet child? *(Answers will vary.)*

5. Do you think Goldilocks is trying to land in the water? If so, why would she want to do this? *(Answers will vary, but possibly to get the cats wet.)*

6. Have you ever seen or used a phone like the one Goldilocks' mother is using? *(Answers will vary.)*

7. When Goldilocks enters the forest, what does the illustration remind you of? *(Answers will vary; possibly a game.)*

8. What kind of house does the bear's house look like? *(Possibly a gingerbread house.)*

9. Would anyone today put on a hat and glasses to ride on a bicycle? Why do you think they did it then? *(Answers will vary.)*

10. Before Goldilocks eats the porridge, the story says: "On the dining room table were three inviting bowls of porridge." What does this mean? *(Answers will vary. They were asking her to eat them.)*

11. Who is Goldilocks talking to when she says, "I don't mind if I do"? *(Answers will vary.)*

12. Goldilocks cries out "Patooie!" What does this mean? *(Answers will vary.)*

13. How do you think the big bowl of porridge got spilled? *(Answers will vary.)*

Lesson 2

The story may be divided at this point to avoid a terribly long lesson.

14. Why would Goldilocks think the coarse brown fur belonged to kitties? *(Kittens are more likely to be found in a house.)*

15. What do you think the initials P.B. mean on the back of the large greenish chair? *(Papa Bear.)*

16. How did Goldilocks break the little chair? *("She rocked and rocked until the chair fell completely to pieces!")*

17. What does it mean when it says Goldilocks was quite "tuckered out"? *(She was very tired.)*

18. What was wrong with the first bed? *(The head was much too high.)*

19. What was wrong with the next bed? *(The head was much too low.)*

20. Do you think all three bears read a lot in bed? *(The number of books beside each bed seems to indicate that they do.)*

21. What does Baby Bear mean when he says his chair was broken to "smithereens"? *(It was really broken!)*

22. Why did the bears tiptoe upstairs? *(They did not know what they might find.)*

23. How did Papa Bear react to someone having been in his bed? *(He was not happy.)*

24. What did Mama Bear mean when she said "Egads!" *(Answers will vary.)*

25. Did the three Bears ever speak to Goldilocks? *(Apparently not.)*

CONCLUDING CRITICAL THINKING EXERCISES

1. This story is written from the point of view of the narrator. Rewrite the story from the point of view of one of the bears.

2. Create an original character and tell how the character would fit into the book.

3. Write new lyrics to a known tune and retell the story of *Goldilocks and the Three Bears.*

4. Obtain other copies of this story. Compare each in relation to setting (where and when the story takes place), the story line and sequence, the end of the story, and the illustrations.

5. Rewrite the end of the story.

6. Do you think Goldilocks was punished for disobeying or do you think she learned a lesson from her experiences?

7. Compare the illustrations in this book with those of another book with the same title. Discuss why this book was chosen as a Caldecott Honor Book. Be able to defend or justify your reasons.

8. Use the general theme of this book and rewrite it using rock stars or some other type of character.

9. Write to the author and illustrator of this book and explain your reaction to how he updated the story line. Justify all your reasons.

CONCLUDING EXTENSION ACTIVITIES

Suggestions for specific as well as general activities that can be used with this book follow. A complete list of general activities can be found at the end of the book.

1. Make sentence strips of the story. Cut the strips apart and then see if someone in the group can reassemble them in the correct sequential order.

2. Make a list of as many stories as you can find about bears. Put them in two groups—true stories about bears (non-fiction) and bear stories that could not possibly be true (fiction). You may start the fiction group with this book.

3. Make a project cube of the story. Before folding it into a cube, draw six different scenes from the story.

4. Create a cartoon telling the story of *Goldilocks and the Three Bears.*

5. Rewrite and dramatize the story as a puppet show. You will need a narrator, Goldilocks, Papa Bear, Mama Bear, and Baby Bear. Make finger puppets to act out the story.

6. Make a bulletin board about the book.

7. Obtain a copy of *Goldilocks and the Three Bears in Signed English.* This particular book is printed by Gallaudet College Press, Washington D.C. The adaption is by Karen Luczak Saualiner and illustrations by Ralph R. Miller. Learn how to tell the story in sign language. After you feel you are good at it, tell it in sign language to some students or adults who are deaf and who use sign language all the time.

8. Make a chart or poster so that others will want to read this version of *Goldilocks and the Three Bears.*

OTHER BOOKS BY JAMES MARSHALL

George and Martha. Boston: Houghton, 1972.

George and Martha Encore. Boston: Houghton, 1973.

Red Riding Hood. Dial, 1987.

Cinderella. Boston: Houghton, 1989.

Hansel and Gretel. Boston: Houghton, 1990.

Hey, Al

Written by Arthur Yorinks

Illustrated by Richard Egielski

New York: Farrar, Straus, and Giroux, 1986

Reading Level: 3   **Interest Level: K–3**

Author

Arthur Yorinks was born on August 21, 1953, in Roslyn, New York. He attended New School for Social Research and Hofstra New College. He continues to live in the New York area. During his career, he has been an instructor in theatre arts at Cornell University and a writer, teacher, and performer at the American Mime Theatre.

Illustrator

Richard Egielski was born on July 16, 1952, in New York, N.Y. He studied at Pratt Institute and the Parsons School of Design. He claims that cartoons were his first influence in art. Books were not an important part of his early life. He attended parochial school until high school and he felt that all creativity was stifled there. It wasn't until he attended the High School of Art and Design that self-expression was emphasized. It wasn't until after this point that he considered art as a career.

Maurice Sendak played an important part in his life. Sendak was not only one of Egielski's most important teachers, but he put him in touch with Arthur Yorinks, with whom he continues to collaborate.

Synopsis

Al and his dog, Eddie, became very unhappy with their life in a one-room apartment. One night a big bird appeared and offered to change their lives. Al, afraid at first, decided to go with the bird. They were taken to a bird paradise. Everything was beautiful and the two were very happy until they began turning into birds themselves. They flew back to their apartment and decided things weren't so bad after all.

This story could be classified as a modern fable. There are two stated morals: "Ripe fruit soon spoils" and "Paradise lost is sometimes Heaven found." The implied moral "The grass is always greener on the other side of the fence" is also present in this story.

Theme or Central Thought

1. Use of animals to portray human qualities.

2. The grass is always greener on the other side.

3. Be satisfied with what you have.

Literary Objectives

1. The student will be able to analyze characters, their traits, motives, and feelings, and compare the characters to themselves.

2. The student will be able to compare and contrast what really happens to what cannot happen (real and unreal).

3. The student will be able to evaluate characters' actions.

DISCUSSION QUESTIONS

Lesson 1

1. The use of color is quite noticeable in this book. Why do you think the room Al and his dog live in is portrayed in drab colors? *(Answers may vary.)*

2. Describe how you think they live. Would you be happy to live this way? *(Answers may vary.)*

3. When the big bird sticks his head through the bathroom window, what shows you Al might be frightened? *(Answers may vary, but the expression on his face and dropping his razor might be two items.)*

4. In the next picture of Al sitting on his suitcase holding a feather, where do you think the feather came from? *(Possibly the big bird.)*

5. As the large bird is taking Al and his dog to their new destination, what happens? *(Al drops his suitcase.)*

6. By looking at the next few full-page illustrations, tell how Al and his dog like their new home. *(Answers will vary.)*

7. What problem arises? *(They develop wings and beaks.)*

8. Why do you think Al is painting the room in the last picture? *(Answers may vary, but certainly the fact that they want to make their living conditions better should come up.)*

Lesson 2

Vocabulary words that may need to be explained:

janitor	plenty	pigeons	struggling
confused	conversation	down	ferried
lush	gorgeous	flitted	to and fro
cascaded	cooed	blissfully	ecstasy
shrieked	honked	squawked	frenzy
exhausted	aloft	talented	paradise

1. What did Al do for a living? *(Al was a janitor.)*

2. On the first page, there is something written that indicates there is a problem. What does it say? *("What could be bad?")*

3. Who was unhappier with their situation, Al or Eddie? *(Eddie.)*

4. When and where did the big bird appear? *(One morning the big bird stuck his head in the bathroom window.)*

5. What did Eddie mean when he said, "There's more to life than mops and pails!"? *(Answers will vary.)*

6. Do you think that dropping the suitcase is going to have any effect on the story? *(Answers will vary.)*

7. Are the birds on the island real birds or make-believe birds? *(Answers may vary, but most look real while others look make-believe.)*

8. Are the birds happy with their new visitors? *(They seem to be.)*

9. Name some of the things Al will be eating while on the island. *(Coconut milk, apples, bananas, grapes, oranges, and possibly fish.)*

10. What were some of the bird characteristics that began to appear on Eddie and Al? *(Eyes were beady, noses beak-like, wings sprouted, tail feathers appeared.)*

11. What is the attitude of the other birds? Why? Be specific. *(Suddenly, they are turning their backs on Al and Eddie. Answers will vary as to why, but make sure each is substantiated.)*

12. What did Al think had happened to Eddie? *(He had dropped into the ocean and possibly drowned.)*

13. How was Al feeling about the loss of Eddie? *("Heartbroken.")* Did his heart really break? *(No.)*

14. What do you see in the picture where Al is on the floor that indicates they were at the island in the sky for several days? *(Newspapers outside the door.)*

15. How did Eddie get back? *(He was a very good swimmer.)*

16. What does the last line of the story mean? *(Answers may vary.)*

CONCLUDING CRITICAL THINKING EXERCISES

1. Make a "T Diagram" and distinguish between what could be real in *Hey, Al* and what could not possibly be real.

2. Why do you think *Hey, Al* was chosen as a Caldecott Award book?

3. Discuss, act out, or rewrite this book making all the characters real people like Al.

4. Create an original character or animal and tell how it would fit into the story.

5. Make four categories—Funniest Part, Saddest Part, Happiest Part, Most Believable Part—and list something from the story in each category.

CONCLUDING EXTENSION ACTIVITIES

Suggestions for specific as well as general activities that can be used with this book follow. A complete list of general activities can be found at the end of the book.

1. Write new lyrics to a known tune and retell the story in the song.

2. Make a "WANTED" poster for Eddie that could have been used if he hadn't returned.

3. At the end of this book, Al is painting his room. Choose a room in your house and tell what you would like to do to make it look better.

4. Discuss what characteristics make an island. Tell about an island you have seen or one on which you have been.

5. Use the sample form included in the back of this book and make a story map.

6. Conduct a survey of your classmates as to how they liked this book. Make a graph of your results.

7. Write newspaper stories and advertisements telling about the book and why parents should buy it for their children.

8. Fold a large piece of paper into eight sections. Write or draw a different part of the story in each section.

9. Make finger puppets of all the characters and animals, then act out the story.

10. Draw a picture of your favorite bird and then list a few of its characteristics.

OTHER BOOKS BY ARTHUR YORINKS AND RICHARD EGIELSKI

Sid and Sol. New York: Farrar, Straus, 1977.

Louis the Fish. New York: Farrar, Straus, 1980.

It Happened in Pinsk. New York: Farrar, Straus, 1983.

Lon Po Po

Translated and Illustrated by Ed Young

New York: Philomel Books, 1989

Reading Level: 3   Interest Level: K–4

Author

Ed Young was born on November 28, 1931, in Tientsin, China. He attended City College of San Francisco, the University of Illinois, the Art Center College of Design, and Pratt Institute. His career has included being an illustrator and designer and an instructor in visual communications at Pratt Institute as well as freelance work. Young is an instructor in Tai Chi Chuan (a Chinese exercise) he describes as "a form of moving meditation which is beneficial to mind and body; the whole of the person." He became a director of the Shr Jung Tai Chi Chuan School in New York's Chinatown.

Synopsis

One day a woman had to leave her three children to go to visit their grandmother. She warned her children to close and latch the door when she left. Shortly, there came a knock by someone claiming to be their Granny, their Po Po. This, of course, was the wolf dressed in disguise. They let him in, but the oldest child soon realized the deception and had to find a way to get herself and her sisters out of danger.

Theme or Central Thought

1. Good versus evil.

2. Cleverness.

3. Overcoming obstacles.

Literary Objectives

1. The student will be able to evaluate and analyze a character's actions.

2. The student will be able to compare and contrast different stories with the same theme.

3. The student will be able to understand elements of a story.

Before Reading

Before studying this book, read one of the more familiar renditions of this story to the students. This will familiarize the students with the general plot and enable them to compare the same plot in different settings.

Lesson 1

The illustrations in this book are in the form of Chinese panels. Each picture is an extension of the one before. Panel art is a technique that was begun in ancient China.

First illustration (before the story begins): Can you see Grandma and the wolf in this picture?

Picture 1: Who do you think that is in the large panel picture? *(Mother?)* The children are in the middle.

Picture 2: What feeling do you get in the second picture? *(Dark colors usually indicate fear.)*

Picture 3: What do you think stands out in the wolf? *(Answers will vary. It could be his eye, nose or teeth.)*

Picture 4: How is the wolf represented? *(Black shadow.)*

Picture 5: Describe this picture and how it makes you feel. *(Answers will vary.)*

Picture 6: What is represented in this picture? Why do *you* think the eye stands out so much? *(Answers will vary.)*

Picture 7: This picture shows more light colors than dark. Why do you think the illustrator did this? *(Try to lead the children to think that perhaps good things are going to happen from here on.)*

Picture 8: What does the green represent in this picture? *(Leaves of a tree.)* Where is the wolf? *(Below the tree.)*

Picture 9: What do you think the wolf is doing? *(Answers will vary.)*

Picture 10: This illustration is actually two pictures. In the first, the children are pulling the wolf up the tree. Why do you think they are doing this? What is happening next? *(The wolf is falling.)*

Picture 11: How do you explain the next picture? *(The wolf is again pulled up—higher this time—and again falls.)*

Picture 12: Describe what you think is happening on these pages. *(Point out the hands above the rope.)* What do you think the hands mean?

Picture 13: Describe the children's feelings. *(Answers will vary.)*

Picture 14: The last panel ends the story. Do you think it has a happy ending or not? *(Answers will vary.)*

DISCUSSION QUESTIONS

Lesson 1

In discussing this story, each group of panels will be discussed together, but they will be referred to as Panel 1, Panel 2, etc.

Panel 1:

1. How old do you think the children are? *(Answers will vary.)*

2. Do you think the children look old enough to be left alone overnight? *(Answers will vary.)*

3. What time were the children supposed to lock the door? *(Answers may vary. The story does not say exactly; says to lock it at sunset. Since it is probably summer because of the leaves on the tree, sunset could be 8 or 9 o'clock.)*

Panel 2:

Vocabulary:

      dusk   disguised   jewels

1. When is dusk? *(Not quite dark.)*

2. What does Po Po mean? *(Granny.)*

3. Are the children afraid at this point? *(Answers may vary.)*

4. What is the name of the oldest girl? *(Shang.)*

Panel 3:

Vocabulary:

journey

1. Do the children think this is really their grandmother? *(At this point, they probably do.)*

Panel 4:

Vocabulary:

caught   cunning wolf

1. Who opened the door and let the wolf in the house? *(Tao and Paotze—they were excited to see their grandmother.)*

2. Do you think Shang thinks something might be wrong? Why? *(The wolf blew out the candle.)*

Panel 5:

Vocabulary:

embraced   stretched   touched

1. Shang noticed several things that she questioned. What are these things? *(First the late arrival; then the low voice; then he immediately blew out the candle; wolf's bushy tail and hands with thorns on them.)*

Panel 6:

Vocabulary:

hemp   awl   hairy

1. Does the story help explain the picture on this page? *(Bright eye probably is when Shang turns on the light.)*

2. What did Shang mean when she said, "Po Po, Po Po, your hand has thorns on it"? *(There are claws on his paws.)*

Panel 7:

Vocabulary:

gingko nut   sigh   delighted

1. Do you think there is really a gingko nut? *(Answers may vary.)* Does it matter? *(No, because the wolf didn't know.)*

2. Shang was clever enough to make a promise about the nut. What was that? *(You would live forever.)*

3. What other way was Shang clever? *(She said the nuts were on the top, knowing the wolf could not climb the tree.)*

Panel 8:

Vocabulary:

pluck

1. Is the wolf suspicious? *(He does not seem to be.)*

2. When are the nuts magic? *(Only when they are plucked directly from the tree.)*

Panel 9:

Vocabulary:

paced   eldest   clever

1. How do you know what the wolf is doing in the picture? *(The illustration probably represents the wolf's mouth watering for a taste of the gingko nut.)*

2. From looking at all the illustrations, do you think the wolf will get to the nuts? *(Answers will vary.)*

Panel 10:

Vocabulary:

fetched   pretended

1. How did the wolf fall? *(Shang let go of the rope.)*

2. Do you think the wolf will make it next time? *(Answers may vary.)*

Panel 11:

Vocabulary:

furious   cursed

1. Why was the wolf mad? *(He didn't get to the top again.)*

2. Do you think the wolf is suspicious yet? Why? *(No, if he were suspicious, he wouldn't try again.)*

Panel 12:

Vocabulary:

hei yo

1. Does the song the children were singing remind you of another song? *("Hi ho, hi ho, it's off to work we go" from* Snow White and the Seven Dwarfs.)

2. What was the cue for the girls to let go? *(Shang coughed!)*

3. What do you think "he broke his heart to pieces" means? *(Answers may vary, but elicit that he died.)*

Panel 13:

Vocabulary:

latch

1. The children went back in the house and "fell peacefully asleep." Do you think you could do this? *(Answers will vary.)*

Panel 14:

1. Do you think Mother believed the children? *(Answers may vary.)*

2. Could their story have been made up? *(Answers will vary.)*

3. How could they have proved it was the truth? *(The dead wolf and the basket.)*

CONCLUDING CRITICAL THINKING EXERCISES

1. There were three children. Who was oldest, middle, and youngest? *(Shang oldest, Tao middle, Paotze youngest.)* Justify your answer.

2. Compare this Red Riding Hood story to the one we know. What is the same? What is different?

3. Describe how you think the younger children feel about their older sister. Justify your answer by giving examples.

4. Do you think *Lon Po Po* is a good title for this book. Justify your answer. *(The story does not tell that Lon means wolf. The title* Lon Po Po *means "Granny Wolf.")*

5. Think of another original way to get rid of or trick the wolf.

6. Give a recommendation as to why *Lon Po Po* should be read. Give good reasons for your recommendations.

7. Write new lyrics to a known tune and retell the story of *Lon Po Po.*

8. Compare the artwork in this book with the artwork in other books by Ed Young. Are they the same? What is your opinion of the reason for this?

9. Write a letter to Ed Young, the translator and illustrator at the publishing company. Explain your reactions to his illustrations in this book. Justify your reasons.

10. Extend and write an original ending to *Lon Po Po.*

CONCLUDING EXTENSION ACTIVITIES

1. Make a picture dictionary of some of the nouns in this book. Be sure to include "gingko tree."

2. Use any type of clay or play dough and make a sculpture of the wolf.

3. Design an original book cover for *Lon Po Po.*

4. Draw and make a comic book of *Lon Po Po* that could be enjoyed by very young children.

5. Read *Lon Po Po* on a cassette tape so that younger children can enjoy it.

6. Make a diorama of one of the scenes of this book.

7. Research the gingko tree and write a report on it.

8. Rewrite this book as a play or a puppet show.

9. The illustrations in this book were done with a mixture of watercolors and pastels (chalk). Try to make a picture using these same media.

OTHER BOOKS ILLUSTRATED BY ED YOUNG

Lewis, Elizabeth F. *Young Fu of the Upper Tangtze.* new edition, New York: Holt, 1973.

Root, Phyllis. *Moon Tiger.* New York: Rinehart & Winston, 1985.

Wilde, Oscar. *Oscar Wilde's The Happy Prince.* Englewood Cliffs, N.J.: Prentice-Hall, 1989.

Louie, Ai-Ling. *Yeh Shen: A Cinderella Story from China.* New York: Philomel Books, 1982.

May I Bring a Friend?

by Beatrice Schenk de Regniers

Illustrated by Beni Montresor

New York: Atheneum, 1964

Reading Level: 2–4   Interest Level: K–3

Author

Beatrice Schenk de Regniers, author of many outstanding books for children (including some notable award-winners such as this one), was born on August 16, 1914, in Lafayette, Indiana. Her education took place at the University of Illinois, University of Chicago, and Winnetka Graduate Teachers College. Her career began as a director of educational materials. She has also been editor of Lucky Book Club for Scholastic Book Services.

Illustrator

Beni Montresor, a widely acclaimed artist from Verone, designs stage sets, opera sets, costumes, as well as illustrates wonderful books for children. He was born on March 31, 1926, in Italy and came to the United States in 1960. In Italy, he was a newspaper film critic and author of radio plays, and did adaptions of children's fairy tales.

Synopsis

A young boy visits the Royal Family several times. Each visit he asks if he can bring a friend. Each friend turns out to be an animal friend, and each visit brings a different friend.

Theme or Central Thought

1. Development of friendships.
2. Use of animals to portray human qualities (personification).

Literary Objectives

1. The student will be able to evaluate a character's actions on the choices he makes.

2. The student will be able to recognize the rhyming that takes place in the story.

3. The student will be able to compare and contrast friendships of the main character.

DISCUSSION QUESTIONS

Lesson 1

May I Bring a Friend? was the winner of the 1965 Caldecott Award. Lesson 1 will probably extend over two sessions.

1. What could be more natural than a child asking "May I bring a friend?" when invited to do anything? Discuss times when students have asked this question of an adult.

2. Skim through the book and make generalizations about the illustrations. The following points might be brought out: Some pictures are in one color, some have no color (these are usually not whole page pictures), some use pen-and-ink techniques, and some are multicolored and bright.)

3. Look at the first picture. What can you tell about the story? *(A small boy received a letter; he is standing at the bottom of lots of stairs leading up to a castle.)*

4. Look at the next picture. Who else do you think this story is about? *(A king and queen.)*

5. The next picture is a large, multicolored illustration. What is it that the boy is bringing? *(A giraffe.)*

6. Have you ever seen a giraffe? What color are they really? *(Tan with brown blotches.)*

7. On the next page, the giraffe is sitting at a table. Do you find this a little strange? What can you tell about the story in this picture? *(Answers will vary.)*

8. Look at the next multicolored picture. What is the young boy bringing to the king and queen? *(A hippopotamus.)*

9. What color is a real hippopotamus? *(Gray.)*

10. What is the hippopotamus doing at the table? *(It looks like he's smashing the cake!)*

11. How many monkeys are in the next big picture? *(Twelve.)*

12. How did the king and queen feel about the monkeys? Why? *(Answers may vary, but in the pink picture they look awfully sad, probably because the monkeys are making such a mess of things.)*

13. What is the big animal in the next two-page picture? *(An elephant.)*

14. How did they manage eating with the elephant? *(They sat on the elephant and the elephant's food is on the floor.)*

15. What animals are with the little boy next? How many are there? *(The little boy is with lions. In the first picture there are only seven, but in the pink picture there are eight lions and eight masks.)*

16. What is the last animal to visit the king and queen? *(A seal.)*

17. What can you say about the last big picture? *(Answers will vary, but it will probably be brought out that the king and queen are at a party at the zoo.)*

18. Skim through the book again, looking only at the black-and-white pictures. What can you tell about those? *(Answers may vary. The black-and-white pictures show what the king and queen do together. First they sit on their thrones with a black kitten; next they pick flowers; they dance in the palace; they fish together; they catch butterflies; the king pushes the queen in a swing; and they roll yarn into a ball.)*

Lesson 2

Read the book aloud and elicit predictions based on the illustrations.

Emphasize the rhyming and the repetition of the two stanzas ending with "Any friend of our friend is welcome here." These stanzas are not always the exact same words, but they mean the same. Encourage the students to join in on the repetitive parts.

Next, have the students read the book in unison with you. This is a fun book for children to read together.

Eventually some of the children will want to try to read the story alone. If they make small mistakes, do not correct them as long as the meaning does not change.

Vocabulary and/or expressions that might need discussion:

Opposite picture with giraffe: "Fancy meeting you!"

After hippopotamus: "The King and Queen sent me a *card.*"

With monkeys: "And said, 'What monkey business is this?' "

With seal: "Let's hear you play Oh-Say-Can-You-See." What are they talking about? *(The National Anthem.)*

CONCLUDING CRITICAL THINKING EXERCISES

1. Compare the illustrations in this book with those in another book. Discuss why this book might have been chosen as a Caldecott Award winner. Students should be able to defend or justify their answers.

2. Think of another animal that you could take. Why would you choose that particular animal? Can you think of a rhyme that would be consistent with the rest of the book?

3. Use the general theme of this book and rewrite it using rock stars, or some other type of friend, to take to visit the king and queen.

4. If you were invited to tea with a king and queen and you could take only one friend, who or what would it be? Why?

5. Have a group discussion concerning whether this book would make a good TV show. Would you have to add some more to it? What other animals could be added? Brainstorm and then select the best answers.

6. Imagine you are the little boy and that you have to convince your family that you really are invited to have tea with a king and queen and you can bring a friend. How would you go about it?

7. Write to the illustrator and explain your reaction to his illustrations in the book.

8. Pretend you are a famous child actor and you have been asked to play the part of the little boy. Will you play the part? Explain your answer, yes or no.

9. Write any kind of an original poem about the book.

CONCLUDING EXTENSION ACTIVITIES

Suggestions for specific as well as general activities that can be used with this book follow. A complete list of general activities can be found at the end of the book.

1. Rewrite *May I Bring A Friend?* into a play format and act it out for your class.

2. Reproduce the Story Mapping outline on large chart paper. If the children are advanced enough, give each a small copy to fill out at the same time.

3. Choose two or three of the black and white pictures and redo them in color.

4. Use a scene in the book and illustrate it in one color and again in different colors.

5. Create an original character or animal and tell how it would fit into the story.

6. Design a new and original book cover for this book.

7. Make a "thumbprint" book about *May I Bring A Friend?* (the figures come from thumbs dipped in paint) and write captions for these illustrations.

8. Design a bulletin board about this book. Have an adult help you draw really big pictures to cut out and use on your bulletin board.

9. Create a colorful mural on the chalkboard or on a long piece of paper telling the whole story.

10. Use any type of clay or play dough and make a sculpture of one of the animals in *May I Bring a Friend?*.

OTHER BOOKS BY BEATRICE DE REGNIERS

Jack and the Beanstalk. N.Y.: Atheneum, 1985.

So Many Cats! N.Y.: Clarion Books, 1985.

The Way I Feel . . . Sometimes. N.Y.: Clarion Books, 1988.

The Snow Party. N.Y.: Lothrop, Lee & Shepard Books, 1989.

OTHER BOOKS ILLUSTRATED BY BENI MONTRESOR

Stolz, Mary. *Belling the Tiger.* (Newbery Honor book) N.Y.: Harper, 1962.

I Saw a Ship a-Sailing. N.Y.: Knopf, 1967.

On Christmas Eve. N.Y.: Harper & Row, 1985.

Rumpelstiltskin

Retold and Illustrated by
Paul O. Zelinsky

New York: Dutton, 1986

Reading Level: 2   **Interest Level: K–3**

Author

Paul Zelinsky was born on February 14, 1953, in Evanston, Illinois. He was educated at Yale University and the Tylor School of Art. He now lives in Brooklyn, New York, with his wife, Deborah, and daughter, Anna. He has always made his living as an artist, author, and illustrator of books for children. He has also teamed up with Beverly Cleary as illustrator for some of her books *(Ralph S. Mouse* and *Dear Mr. Henshaw).*

Synopsis

This is the tale of the beautiful daughter of the poor miller. In trying to impress the king, the miller claims his daughter can spin straw into gold. She does not have the slightest idea how to spin straw into gold, but is given help by "a little man" in return for her firstborn child.

The illustrations are in oil and representative of the late medieval setting. The illustrations actually look like they were done in medieval times instead of in 1986. It is easy to understand why this book was a Caldecott Honor book.

Themes or Central Thought

1. There is danger in falsifying the abilities of oneself or another.

2. Lying is usually detected.

3. Truthfulness always wins out.

Literary Objectives

1. The student will be able to develop an appreciation of folklore and storytelling of fairy tales.

2. The student will be able to identify elements of a fairy tale, such as an unbelievable story with good and bad characters as well as brave and timid ones.

3. The student will be able to analyze folklore and compare the same theme in differing countries. (The teacher might want to obtain the additional books listed at the end.)

DISCUSSION QUESTIONS

Lesson 1

Before reading the story in the book, leaf through the book and let the illustrations tell the story. In this way the children can predict what the story is about and how the plot is solved. After reading, they will see how close they were in their predictions to the actual story.

1. Compare the dress of the daughter before and after her marriage to the king. *(Answers will vary, but she seems to wear the same type of clothes before and after her marriage to the king.)*

2. In the second illustration, why do you suppose Mr. Zelinsky shows no wall on one side of the castle? Do you think this is really how the castle is? *(Answers will vary, but he probably did it this way so that the reader could see inside the castle.)*

3. Is there anything at the beginning of the story that might indicate that "the little man" is not a good person? *(Answers will vary.)*

4. In the wedding picture, what strikes you as being strange? *(Answers will vary; however, the dog seems to be out of place.)*

5. Why do you think the queen has the strange expression on her face after she has a baby? *(Answers will vary.)*

6. What do you think the dark pictures represent? *(Fear.)*

7. Why do you think the illustrator used a full moon in the dark picture? *(Possibly so that the characters could be seen.)*

8. Do you think this story has a happy ending? Why? *(In the last illustration, the queen has a smile on her face.)*

Lesson 2

Vocabulary:

miller	encountered	impress	straightaway
intrigued	slightest	frightened	weep
sprang	amazed	delighted	rejoiced
gasped	scarcely	demanded	piteously
inquiries	imagine	shrieked	

Because of the vocabulary, it might be wise for an adult to read this story to younger children first and let the children follow along. Most of the above words are easily defined when read in context.

1. Why did the miller tell the king his daughter could spin straw into gold? *(The miller must have known of the king's love for gold and, consequently, wanted to impress the king.)*

2. Why do you think the daughter was threatened with death if she could not spin the straw into gold? *(Answers will vary.)*

3. When the king left, he locked the door, but the little man was still able to get in. How do you think this happened? *(Answers will vary.)*

4. What was the thing the miller's daughter first gave the little man so that he would spin for her? *(Her necklace.)*

5. How did the gold affect the king? *(He was delighted and amazed, but it only made him want more.)*

6. What word tells you that the king wanted more? *(Greedier.)*

7. How did the king again threaten the miller's daughter? *(With her life.)*

8. What did the daughter give the little man this time? *(The ring on her finger.)*

9. The third time the king did not threaten her life. What did he do instead? *(He said she would become his wife.)*

10. What did the little man demand this time? *(He wanted her first child when she was queen.)*

11. Under what condition did the little man say she could keep her baby? *(He gave her three days to know his name.)*

12. How did the queen finally learn his name? *(She sent her most trusted servant to spy on him.)*

13. Who did the little man think told her his name? *(The devil.)*

14. Did the little man ever bother her again? *(No.)*

CONCLUDING CRITICAL THINKING EXERCISES

1. Do you think the king was in love with the miller's daughter? Give reasons why or why not. *(He threatened her life if she didn't spin gold.)*

2. Compare and contrast this book with the Caldecott Award book *Duffy and the Devil* retold by Harve Zemach and illustrated by Margot Zemach.

3. If the story of *Rumpelstiltskin* were to have a lesson such as fables do, what could the lesson be? Think of one that would be appropriate and be able to defend why you think that would be the lesson.

4. Write an original story with the same plot as *Rumpelstiltskin.* You can use a modern setting if you prefer.

5. Pretend you have to convince a group of parents to buy this book for their children. Give reasons as to why they should buy it.

6. Compose three new titles for this story that would give the reader an idea of what the story is about.

7. The little man sings a song about his name. Write new lyrics to a known tune to retell this story in the song.

CONCLUDING EXTENSION ACTIVITIES

1. Make sentence strips of the story. Cut the strips apart and then see if someone else in the group can regroup the strips in the correct sequential order.

2. Make a "WANTED" poster for the little man.

3. This story was originally told by the Grimm brothers. Do some research on Grimms' fairy tales and write a report on them.

4. Rewrite *Rumpelstiltskin* as a puppet show. Make finger puppets and then put on the play for a class.

5. Make a time line of the events in the life of the miller's daughter. This should be in the correct order.

6. Make a chart or poster so that others will want to read this book. Make it as colorful as possible.

7. Make a diorama of one of the scenes of the story.

8. Use any type of clay or play dough to make a sculpture of one of the characters in this book.

9. Fold a large piece of paper into six or eight sections. Write or draw a different part of the story on each section. Be sure they are in the right order.

ADDITIONAL READINGS WITH THE SAME THEME

Belpré, Pure. *Oté: A Puerto Rican Folktale.* Illustrated by Paul Galdone. New York: Pantheon, 1969.

Zemach, Harve. *Duffy and the Devil.* Illustrated by Margot Zemach. New York: Farrar, Straus, and Giroux, 1986.

Saint George and the Dragon

Retold by Margaret Hodges
Illustrated by Trina Schart Hyman
Boston: Little, Brown and Company, 1984

Reading Level: 4   Interest Level: 2–6

Author

Margaret Moore Hodges was born on July 26, 1911, in Indianapolis, Indiana; she married Fletcher Hodges, Jr., September 10, 1932. She has three children, Fletcher III, Arthur Carlisle, and John Andrews. She received her B.A. at Vassar College with honors in 1932. Her M.L.S. was attained at Carnegie Institute of Technology. She was children's librarian at Carnegie Library of Pittsburgh from 1953 to 1964. Her hobbies and other interests include traveling, reading, folklore and gardening.

Illustrator

Trina Schart Hyman was born in Philadelphia, Pennsylvania, and decided at an early age that she wanted to be an artist. She first studied art in high school and continued her training at the Boston Museum School of Fine Arts. She won the Boston Globe/Horn Book Award in 1973 for her illustrations in *King Stork* written by Howard Pyle. In 1982, her *Rapunzel* was selected as an A.L.A. Notable Book, and in 1984 her edition of *Little Red Riding Hood* was a Caldecott Honor Book and won the Golden Kite Award for illustration. She was also the first art director for *Cricket Magazine.* Much of her work is framed in the delicate floral or geometric patterns that are so outstanding in *Saint George and the Dragon.*

Synopsis

Hodges retells a portion of the legend from Edmund Spencer's *The Faerie Queene* in which George, the Red Cross Knight, slays the dreadful dragon that has been frightening the people of the countryside for years, and thus brings happiness and peace to them.

He marries Una, daughter of the king of the land, and is promised the kingdom after he completes his promise of service to the Fairy Queen for six years.

Theme or Central Thought

1. Celebration of life.

2. Role of courage in the face of conflict.

3. Maintaining perseverance.

4. Good versus evil.

Literary Objectives

1. The student will be able to develop an awareness and appreciation of legends from different lands. This book presents beautiful pictures of the English medieval countryside.

2. The student will be able to recognize the elements and characteristics of folklore, particularly good versus evil.

3. The student will be able to identify relationships between characters.

DISCUSSION QUESTIONS

Lesson 1

Because of the content and beautiful illustrations of this book, it is suggested that the teacher first read this book to the students in order to ensure continuity and understanding. The individual illustrations will be discussed after this first reading, along with the story itself.

Lesson 2

This lesson runs through page 13. No particular attention should be given to individual vocabulary words before reading. They will, however, be listed. Encourage students to try to understand the words by making guesses from the context of the whole sentence.

Vocabulary:

shield	dented	veiled	clock
frightened	champion	perils	thorny
hermit	glorious	plowman	brassy

1. In each corner of page 7, there is a shield with a red cross. Read to find out why it was dented. (*"It was dented with the blows of many battles fought long ago by other brave knights."*)

2. Why do you think the face of the princess was covered? *(Answers will vary, the story doesn't say.)*

3. What was the name of the princess? *(Una.)*

4. What was the knight called? *(Red Cross Knight.)* Why do you think he was called this? *(His shield was decorated with a red cross.)*

5. What do you see in each corner on page 8? *(A dragon.)*

6. Why do you think the path was not easy to see? *(Answers will vary, but from the picture, it looks very wooded, like a forest.)*

7. What did the Red Cross Knight do while Una rested? *(He and the hermit climbed to the top of the hill and looked out across the valley.)*

8. Why couldn't the Red Cross Knight and Una go to the High City? *(The High City was in another world and the Fairy Queen had sent the knight to do brave deeds in this world first.)*

9. In the picture on page 14, describe why everyone seems to be cheering. *(They knew a champion had come to fight the dragon.)*

10. Explain the knight's birth and what happened to him afterward. *(He was born of English earth; the fairies stole him and hid him in a farmer's field. A plowman found him and called him George.)*

11. Why was the knight called George? *(It means "Plow the Earth" and "Fight the Good Fight.")*

12. What was he born to be? *(England's friend and patron saint, Saint George of Merry England.)*

Lesson 3

This lesson covers pages 14 through 25.

Vocabulary:

hideous	glistening	bade	reared
vast	speckled	devour	sulfur
raging	forth	nostrils	striving
wounded	bellowed	scorched	faint
weary	afar	brandished	smote
lashing	barbed	anvil	severed
brimstone	retreat	stir	furl

1. What is the shadow of the dragon compared to? *(A mountain casting a shadow on a valley.)* (Teacher's note: A simile could be explained at this point.)

2. How do you think George felt when he first saw the dragon? *(Answers will vary.)*

3. Describe the dragon. *(Answers may vary; try to encourage use of the words from the story.)*

4. How did the knight fall off his horse? *(The dragon brushed him with his long tail.)*

5. Do you think the dragon is getting concerned and maybe a little frightened? *(Answers will vary.)*

6. On page 19, what made Una think George had lost the battle? *(The dragon sent a flame that scorched the knight's face and heated his armor, causing him to fall ready to die.)*

7. Why did George cut off the end of the dragon's tail? *(To free himself from it.)*

8. How did the knight sever the dragon's paw? *(The dragon had raised the paw to defend himself and the knight struck it with all his might.)*

9. What do you think the furnace inside the dragon is? *(Answers will vary.)*

10. What emotion allowed the knight to finally kill the dragon? *(The dragon became afraid.)*

Lesson 4

This lesson covers pages 26–32.

Vocabulary

tidings	laurel	wreaths	tambourines
victorious	bolder	embraced	dragonslayer
veil	shimmered	jolly	cargo

1. Describe all the things that happened after the king and queen found out the dragon was dead. *(See page 27.)*

2. What did the children give Una? *(A crown of flowers.)*

3. Why did some of the older men measure the dragon? *(To see how many acres his body covered.)*

4. When the king was giving the knight gifts, what did the knight say? *("Never to forget the poor people. . . .")*

5. Why could the knight not rest and live happily ever after? *(He had sworn his service to the Fairy Queen for six years and could not rest until after that.)*

6. Did the knight have to wait six years to marry Una? *(No, the king said if Una and the knight loved each other the knight could marry her. Then the kingdom would belong to the knight after he did his service to the Fairy Queen.)*

7. What title did the knight earn? *(Saint George of Merry England.)*

8. What do you think is the significance of the last paragraph? *(Answers will vary.)*

CONCLUDING CRITICAL THINKING EXERCISES

1. Describe what kind of person George is and what qualities he has that you wished you had.

2. Explain how George probably felt when he fell beneath the apple tree.

3. Explain how Una felt when she saw George lying motionless under the apple tree.

4. What do you think will probably happen after George completes his six years of service to the Fairy Queen? What kind of king do you think he will make?

5. Could this story be put into modern times? Explain the things that would probably be different. Rewrite the story, giving it a modern setting.

6. Compose three new titles for the story that would give the reader an idea what the story is about.

7. Write lyrics and music to a song that could tell the story of George and the Dragon.

8. This story contains a lot of violence. In your opinion, is it necessary to the content of the story? Defend your position.

CONCLUDING EXTENSION ACTIVITIES

Suggestions for specific as well as general activities that can be used with this book follow. A complete list of general activities can be found at the end of the book.

1. Retell the story from memory as a group. Write this story on the board.

2. This book is filled with similes and metaphors. Skim through the story and write down as many as you can find.

3. What might you do if you had to get rid of a dragon?

4. Make a story map out of this book. (Use the form in the back of the book.)

5. Write out the title decoratively and for each letter write a phrase about the book.

6. Find pictures of as many things as possible that portray the times of knights.

7. If you were going to film this story, what parts would you leave out if you had to leave some out?

8. This book is an excellent choice for puppetry, drama or reader's theater.

OTHER BOOKS ILLUSTRATED BY TRINA SCHART HYMAN

The Castle in the Attic. New York: Holiday House, 1985.

The Canterbury Tales. New York: Lothrop, 1988.

A Connecticut Yankee in King Arthur's Court. New York: Morrow, 1988.

Hershel and the Hanukkah Gobblins. New York: Holiday House, 1989.

Swan Lake. San Diego, Calif.: Harcourt Brace & Jovanovich, 1989.

Sam, Bangs & Moonshine

Written and illustrated by
Evaline Ness

New York: Holt, Rinehart and Winston, 1966

Reading Level: 3   Interest Level: 2–4

Author

Evaline Ness was born on April 24, 1911, in Union City, Ohio. She married Arnold A. Bayard in 1959 and died in Kingston, New York, August 12, 1986, of a heart attack. Her education took place at Ball State Teachers College and Chicago Institute of Art. During her career she was an artist and tapestry designer, as well as an illustrator and author of children's books. Her other interests included Siamese cats and bicycles.

Synopsis

Sam—short for Samantha—was the daughter of a fisherman. They lived alone with Sam's cat, Bangs. Sam's mother had died long ago. Because there were few young people around, Sam lived in her own little world of fantasy, telling stories that even outdid those of the sailors who had been out to sea for a long time. Her father was constantly trying to get her to stop her lying saying, "Today, for a change, talk REAL not MOONSHINE. MOONSHINE spells trouble." When she would ask Bangs what her father meant, Bangs would say, "MOONSHINE is flummadiddle. REAL is opposite." This, of course, made no sense to Sam, and she ended up learning a near-tragic lesson in distinguishing fact from fantasy.

Theme or Central Thought

1. Distinguishing fact from fantasy.

2. Importance of friends.

3. Loyalty.

Literary Objectives

1. The student will be able to recognize the main elements of a story such as plot, characters, and setting.

2. The student will be able to evaluate the character's action in relation to living in an unreal setting and telling lies about it.

3. The student will be able to compare and contrast what is real with what is unreal.

DISCUSSION QUESTIONS

Lesson 1

1. Looking at the illustrations at the beginning of the story, where is the setting of this story? *(Harbor; ocean.)*

2. What is the girl holding opposite the first page? *(Starfish.)*

3. Notice the house near the harbor. How would you describe it?

4. One of the boats in the harbor has the word ARNI on it. Discuss the fact that many boats are named.

5. Notice how all of the illustrations are black, shades of gray, and gold. The only place we see orange is on the cover.

6. Next, we see the girl lying on a rug. Behind her is a character with the top of a woman and the bottom of a fish. Do you know what that's called? *(Mermaid.)*

7. In the illustration of the boy on his bicycle, what does this tell you about the story? *(He could be a friend of the girl, he lives on a farm, etc.—encourage guesses.)*

8. In the next picture, who is in the tree? *(Boy.)* Can you guess why? *(Answers will vary.)*

9. The fences in the next picture represent the snow fences that are sometimes used on a beach—why? *(To keep the sand from eroding.)*

10. Describe the picture of the girl with the dragons. *(Try to elicit that she seems to be in her world of magic.)*

11. Describe the next picture. *(The girl seems to be in deep thought.)* Can you see the boy? *(Far away on his bicycle.)*

12. From this point on, the girl seems very sad for a long time. Can you guess why? *(Answers will vary.)*

13. Find the picture of the lighthouse. Have you seen a real lighthouse? Do they all have stripes? *(Lighthouses have different designs, but don't bring this out now.)*

14. In the next picture, the cat is asleep at the end of the girl's bed. Do you sleep with a real pet?

15. What do you think is hopping on the floor of the next picture? *(Answers will vary.)*

16. Is the animal that the little girl is holding the same animal? *(Answers will vary.)*

17. Looking at the last two pictures in the story, can you predict what happens to the little animal? *(Answers will vary.)*

18. Describe the very last picture.

Lesson 2

This reading goes to the picture of Sam and Bangs sitting on the step—last line: "Pardon me while I go to the moon."

Vocabulary:

reckless	giraffes	mermaid	chariot
scoured	stretched	massive	diminishing

1. Name some of the lies Sam told. *(Sam said her mother was a mermaid when actually she was dead. She said she had a lion and baby kangaroo at home. She claimed her cat could talk and that the rug on the doorstep was a chariot drawn by dragons.)*

2. Explain what you think Sam's father meant when he said: "Today, for a change, talk REAL not MOONSHINE. MOONSHINE spells trouble." *(Answers will vary.)*

3. Who believed everything Sam said? *(Thomas.)* Why do you think he believed her? *(Answers will vary.)*

4. What did Thomas want most to see? *(The baby kangaroo.)*

5. What was the cause for Thomas never being able to see the baby kangaroo? *(Sam always said "it had just stepped out.")*

6. Why do you think Sam told Thomas the story about the baby kangaroo? *(Answers may vary, but it could be that she felt she had a certain power over him.)*

7. Describe some of the places Sam told Thomas the baby kangaroo might be. *(In tall trees visiting owls, in the old windmill grinding corn, in the lighthouse tower warning ships at sea, or asleep on the beach.)*

8. What do you think will probably happen when Thomas goes to the cave behind Blue Rock to hunt for the baby kangaroo? *(Answers will vary; but danger is certain.)*

9. Who do you think really tried to warn Sam of danger? *(Answers will vary.)*

10. Talk about what a tide is and how it goes in and out daily. *(Explanation need not be too specific as there is a research activity on this.)*

Lesson 3

Vocabulary:

stalked	menacing	torrents	murky
oozed	crept	oblong	sodden
smothered	incredible	elegant	gerbil
squealed	laryngitis	immense	wheezed

1. What made Sam suddenly realize what was actually going on? *(Answers will vary, but the weather possibly brought her out of her dream world.)*

2. What does the sentence "Sam stood there looking at nothing, trying to swallow the lump that rose in her throat" mean? *(Answers will vary.)*

3. Describe the weather when Sam's father came home. *(It was raining very hard; water streamed from his hat and oozed from his boots; the rain hammered on the tin roof.)*

4. State the good news and bad news Sam's father had for her. *(Good news was Thomas was okay; bad news was Bangs had not been found.)*

5. Did Sam tell her father the truth about what happened? *(It doesn't say for sure, but the assumption is that she did.)*

6. Do you think Sam will learn a lesson from this or that she will just feel sorry for herself? *(Answers will vary.)*

7. How did Bangs look when he returned? What do you think the word "sodden" means? *(He was all wet. "Sodden" means thoroughly soaked or saturated.)*

8. Did Sam wake her father with the news Bangs had returned? *(No, but he obviously heard something and went to her room.)*

9. What did Sam's father explain about MOONSHINE? *(He said there was good moonshine and bad moonshine; the importance was to know the difference.)*

10. What did Sam think she saw the next morning? What did she really see? *(She thought she saw a baby kangaroo, but it was really a gerbil.)*

11. Why would Thomas not visit her that day? *(He was sick in bed with laryngitis.)*

12. What did Sam do with the gerbil? *(She gave it to Thomas.)*

CONCLUDING CRITICAL THINKING EXERCISES

1. Recall a situation where you did not quite tell the truth, and compare it to this book.

2. Write a letter to Evaline Ness and explain your reaction to her illustrations in this book. Justify your reasons.

3. Think of a new title for this book. Instead of naming the characters in the story, have your title state the main idea of the story.

4. This story was told from the author's point of view. Rewrite this story as if Bangs were telling the story.

5. Rewrite the end of this story.

6. Give reasons why you think this book was chosen as a Caldecott award book. Tell why you agree or disagree with the choice.

7. Pretend you are a famous child actor and have been asked to play the part of Sam in the movie. Would you play the part? (Your answer can be either yes or no, but give reasons for your answer.)

8. Would it make any difference in the story if Sam were a boy instead of a girl? Explain your answer.

CONCLUDING EXTENSION ACTIVITIES

Suggestions for specific as well as general activities that can be used with this book follow. A complete list of general activities can be found at the end of this book.

1. Draw a map of the area where the story takes place.

2. Create a cartoon telling the story in the book. Rewrite it so that a very young child would understand it.

3. Create an original character and tell how the character would fit into the story.

4. Make a cassette tape reading of this book so that a younger child could read-along. Make sure you make a noise of some kind to indicate where the listener should turn the page.

5. Make a picture dictionary of some of the nouns (naming words) in this book.

6. Use the Story Mapping outline and outline the story of *Sam, Bangs & Moonshine*.

7. Fold a large piece of paper into eight sections. In each section write a sentence telling a part of the story. Make sure it is in the correct sequence.

8. Research tides and be able to make a written or an oral report. Be able to explain to your classmates exactly how they work.

9. Research lighthouses and make a written or an oral report.

OTHER BOOKS BY EVALINE NESS

Exactly Alike. New York: Scribner, 1964.

Tom's Tit Tat. New York: Scribner, 1965.

The Girl and the Boatherd or This and That and Thus and So. New York: Dutton, 1970.

Do You Have the Time, Lydia? New York: Dutton, 1971.

Marcella's Guardian Angel. New York: Holiday House, 1979.

Sylvester and the Magic Pebble

By William Steig

New York: Windmill Books, 1969

Reading Level: 3   Interest Level: K–3

Author

William Steig was born on November 14, 1907, in New York, N.Y. His early career was as a cartoonist and it wasn't until the seventh decade of his life that he came into this second profession. He published his first children's book in 1968. He attended City College, New York, and the National Academy of Design.

Synopsis

Sylvester Duncan, a donkey, finds a magic pebble that changes things with the words "I wish." He tests its powers by wishing the weather would change from rain to sun and back again several times. On his way home, he encounters a lion that frightens him. Sylvester panics and says "I wish I were a rock." This, of course, changes him into a rock.

The majority of the story is spent on helping his mother and father look for Sylvester. In the spring, almost a full year later, Mr. and Mrs. Duncan are on a picnic. They have their picnic on the rock that is Sylvester. The magic pebble is beside the rock, and Sylvester's father picks it up and places it on the rock. Sylvester knows his parents are near and wishes he were himself again. And suddenly, he was!

After Sylvester explains the magic pebble to his parents, they immediately put it in an iron safe so that an accident cannot happen again.

Theme or Central Thought

1. Use of animals to portray human qualities.

2. Family struggles.

3. Things are not always what they appear.

Literary Objectives

1. The student will be able to recognize the elements of a story including setting, problem, climax, and ending.

2. The student will be able to recognize the use of personification.

3. The student will be able to evaluate characters' actions.

DISCUSSION QUESTIONS

Lesson 1

1. Do you think this story could really happen? *(No.)*

2. Name as many things as you can in the first picture that you would consider unreal. *(Examples: Donkeys living in a house; Father Donkey smoking a pipe and reading a newspaper; Father Donkey dressed in a suit and tie; Mother Donkey in a dress and sweeping the floor; Sylvester looking at rocks or pebbles while sitting in a chair.)*

3. What do you think is happening in the next two pictures? How are they different? *(Sylvester is looking at a pebble. The difference in the two pictures is that there is rain in the first picture and sun in the second picture. The setting is the same.)*

4. Do donkeys really walk on only their hind legs? *(No.)*

5. Skim through several more pictures. What do you think has happened to Sylvester? *(Answers will vary.)*

6. What kind of animal represents the police? *(Pigs.)* What do you think of this? *(Answers may vary, but some student might bring up the point that some people refer to the police as "pigs.")*

7. What are all the dogs doing? *(Looking for Sylvester.)*

8. What seasons of the year are represented in the illustrations in this book? *(In the beginning it is summer, then fall, winter, and spring in the end.)*

9. What do Mother and Father find on their picnic? *(Sylvester.)*

10. Where do you think he had been? *(Answers will vary at this point.)*

Lesson 2

This lesson will cover the first half of the story (through the picture with all the dogs).

Vocabulary (many meanings can be obtained through context clues):

collecting	extraordinary	unusual	remarkable
shiver	ceased	vanished	gratified
fetlock	gnat	panicked	perplexed
billion	soothe	inquiring	

1. Where did Sylvester live? *(Acorn Road in Oatsdale.)*

2. What was his hobby? *(Collecting pebbles of unusual shape and color.)*

3. How did Sylvester discover the pebble was magic? *(By accident—he wished the rain would stop and it did. Then he tested it by wishing for rain again; it did.)*

4. After changing the weather, what did Sylvester wish? *(He wished a wart on his left fetlock would disappear.)*

5. What caused Sylvester to be frightened? *(A lion.)*

6. What caused Sylvester to turn into a rock? *(He panicked and momentarily forgot the powers of the rock and wished for the wrong thing.)*

7. What should he have done? *(Answers will vary.)*

8. Where is Sylvester in the picture at night? *(Rock.)*

9. List some of the things the Duncans did to try to find Sylvester. *(They asked all the neighbors; talked to all the children; asked the police; all the dogs searched for him.)*

10. How do you think Sylvester will turn back into a donkey? *(Answers will vary.)*

Lesson 3

This lesson covers the last half of the story.

Vocabulary:

concluded	miserable	stone-dumb	aimlessly
alfalfa	loving looks	exclamations	

1. Name some things the Duncans were doing to go about their usual ways. Use the pictures. *(Answers may vary.)*

2. How far away was Sylvester? *(Less than a mile away.)*

3. Did Sylvester give up hope? *(Answers will vary.)*

4. What happened in the winter? *(A wolf sat on Sylvester.)*

5. Point out the magic pebble in the pictures of fall, winter, and spring.

6. When the Duncans go on a picnic, do you get the feeling something special will happen? *(Answers will vary.)*

7. What does it mean when the story says, "He was stone-dumb."? *(Answers will vary. Point out that this is the climax of the story—the part with the most suspense.)*

8. Who found the magic pebble? *(Father.)* Who made the magic wish for Sylvester? *(Sylvester.)*

9. Why is Sylvester crying when Mother is hugging him? *(He is crying because he is so happy. Point out that sometimes we cry for happiness as well as sadness.)*

10. What happened to the magic pebble? *(They put it in an iron safe so that no accidents could happen again.)*

CONCLUDING CRITICAL THINKING EXERCISES

1. Compare the illustrations in this book with those of another book. Discuss why this book might have been chosen as a Caldecott Award book. Students should be able to defend or justify their answers.

2. This book won the Caldecott award in 1970. What if it had been written in 1985, when *Saint George and the Dragon* won the award? Just by comparing the illustrations, do you still think it would have won? Substantiate your answer.

3. What would you have wished if you encountered a lion as Sylvester did?

4. Do you think Mr. and Mrs. Duncan are good parents? Why or why not?

5. What might you do if you found a magic pebble? Write a story telling what would be your very first wish and what you would do with the pebble so it would not be misused.

6. What would you do if Sylvester was your best friend?

7. Write an original poem retelling the story of *Sylvester and the Magic Pebble*.

8. Create an original character and tell how the character would fit into the book.

CONCLUDING EXTENSION ACTIVITIES

Suggestions for specific as well as general activities that can be used with this book follow. A complete list of general activities can be found at the end of the book.

1. Fold a piece of paper into eight sections. Write or draw a different part of the story on each section, retelling the story in the correct sequential order.

2. Create a colorful mural or poster to advertise the book so that others will want to read it.

3. Develop a time line to keep track of the events as they happened.

4. Make a "WANTED" poster for Sylvester so that others who don't know him can also look for him.

5. Design and make a bulletin board about this book.

6. Make finger puppets of all the Duncans, plus some of the other characters, then act out the story.

7. Make a Story Mapping outline on large chart paper. Give each student a small copy to fill out at the same time.

8. When the Duncans have their picnic, they eat strange things. Are these things that donkeys really eat? Do some research and find out what a donkey normally eats.

OTHER BOOKS BY WILLIAM STEIG

Abel's Island. (Newbery Honor Book 1977) New York: Farrar, Straus, 1976.

The Amazing Bone. (Caldecott Honor Book 1977) New York: Farrar, Straus, 1977.

Solomon, the Rusty Nail. New York: Farrar, Straus, 1985.

The Zabajaba Jungle. New York: Farrar, Straus, 1987.

Spinky Sulks. New York: Farrar, Straus, 1988.

The Talking Eggs

by Robert D. San Souci

pictures by Jerry Pinkney

New York: Dial Books for Young Readers, 1989

Reading Level: 4   Interest Level: K–4

Author

Robert D. San Souci was born on October 10, 1946, in San Francisco, California. His career has spanned many areas, most of which have involved books. He has been a book buyer, assistant manager of Campus Textbook Exchange, and consulting editor and author for both adult and children's books. His education took place at St. Mary's College, Moraga, California, where he received his B.A. and he did his graduate work at California State University. Some of his works are with his brother, Daniel, who does illustrations. They share the same birthday, although separated by two years.

Illustrator

Jerry Pinkney was born on December 22, 1939, in Philadelphia, Pennsylvania. He is married to wife Gloria and has three sons and one daughter. He worked as a designer/illustrator for various companies before opening his own studio. He was the designer of the Harriet Tubman, Martin Luther King, Jr., Benjamin Banneker, and Whitney Moore Young, Jr., commemorative stamps for the United States Postal Service's "Black Heritage" series.

Synopsis

This story is about two sisters. Rose is lazy, greedy and spoiled, but favored by the mother. Blanche is sweet, hard-working, and forced to do much work by both the mother and Rose. Blanche finally runs away from home and because of her kindness to an old woman, is befriended by her. The old woman takes Blanche to her home, where Blanche sees all sorts of strange objects. It is here that she sees the talking eggs. Because Blanche does exactly what the old woman says, Blanche is rewarded with all sorts of riches. When her mother and Rose try to duplicate the riches for themselves, they fail because Rose does not do as the old woman says.

This tale is adapted from a Creole folktale brought to the Louisiana area by the French. As with most folktales, it is thought to have its start with oral retellings through the areas.

Theme or Central Thought

1. Kindness is rewarded.

2. Good versus evil.

3. Coping with adversity.

Literary Objectives

1. The student will be able to recognize and understand comparison, particularly with the use of similes (comparisons using "like" or "as") and metaphors (implied comparisons).

2. The student will be able to establish relationships between characters (for example, favorite child, unloved child).

3. The student will be able to recognize characters from different cultures. The characters in this folktale happen to be black and from the American South.

DISCUSSION QUESTIONS

Lesson 1

Read the story to the students before discussing the illustrations.

Illustration 1

1. Why do you suppose there are two happy people and one child working? *(Answers will vary.)*

2. Try to guess how the story will unfold from the first illustration. *(Answers will vary.)*

Illustration 2

1. Where do you think the little girl is going? *(If students don't guess to get water, point out water bucket and ladle.)*

Illustration 3

1. Describe what is happening. *(Mother seems mad. The little girl with pigtails is perhaps scared.)*

2. Why do you think the one girl is throwing out the water from the bucket? *(Answers will vary.)*

Illustration 4

1. Can you tell why the little girl is with the old woman? *(It's doubtful, but encourage guesses.)*

2. Neither is wearing shoes. Why? *(Perhaps they are poor.)*

Illustrations 5 & 6

1. Find all the strange things you can. *(Cows with curly horns; chickens of all colors.)*

2. How would you react if you saw chickens like this? *(Answers will vary.)*

Illustration 7

1. Can you tell what the old woman is doing? *(Answers will vary.)*

Illustration 8

1. Describe the dance.

2. What kind of animals are dancing? *(Rabbits—notice ears sticking out of hats.)*

Illustration 9

1. What is the little girl doing? *(Collecting eggs.)*

2. Describe the eggs she is taking. *(Try to get students to see there are plain eggs and eggs with jewels. She is only taking the plain ones.)*

3. Do you think she will take any of the jeweled ones? *(Answers will vary.)*

Illustrations 10 & 11

1. Describe the square picture. *(The girl is throwing eggs.)*

2. What do you see on the ground? *(Dresses, coins.)*

3. Where do you think the horse and buggy came from? *(Answers will vary.)*

Illustration 12

1. Can you tell what is happening? *(It's doubtful. Write down student responses to compare later when story is read.)*

Illustrations 13 & 14

1. Is this the same old woman? *(Yes.)*

2. What is this girl's reaction? *(Laughter, pointing at the strange things.)*

Illustration 15

1. What do you think is happening? *(Answers will vary.)*

2. What do you think the girl has in her hands? *(Answers will vary. Actually, it's the old woman's head, but this need not be developed at this time, even if it is guessed.)*

Illustration 16

1. What kind of eggs is the girl taking? *(The colorful ones.)*

2. Do you think this is significant? *(Answers will vary.)*

Illustration 17

1. What emotion do you think this picture shows? *(Darkness usually indicates fear.)*

2. How do you think the girl feels? *(Scared.)*

Illustration 18

1. Can you think of one word that might describe this picture? *(Desertion.)*

Lesson 2

There is much figurative language in the form of idioms and expressions peculiar to a region of the American South in this story. Students need to understand these, but not at the expense of actual enjoyment. Since understanding can be accomplished through context, it is not necessary to dissect the story in the beginning. For this reason, treatment of this book will be a little different.

First, read the book to the children for pure enjoyment.

Next, explain that to completely understand the vocabulary it is necessary to isolate some of the words and expressions on each page. Discussion will follow the line of the 15 illustrations.

You might want to explain the following terms at this time:

idiom: an expression normal to a particular place and not to be taken literally.

simile: comparisons using the words like or as.

metaphor: implied comparison, often harder to detect and/or understand.

Lesson 3

Illustration 1

Vocabulary:

window   balls   trail-train

1. What sentence tells you how poor they were? (*"They lived on a farm so poor, it looked like the tail end of bad luck." Elicit that this sounds pretty poor!*)

2. In the second paragraph, Blanche is described as "sharp as forty crickets." Using the balance of the sentence, what would this mean?

3. Discuss "they were alike as two peas in a pod."

4. What do you think "putting on airs" means? (*This might be a good expression to demonstrate.*)

5. What does "fancy balls" mean? (*Formal dances.*)

6. Discuss "wearing trail-train dresses."

Illustration 2

Vocabulary:

fetch

1. "I'm 'bout to die of thirst." This is an idiom; it does not mean she is literally going to die.

2. In some areas of the south, youngsters refer to any elder as "aunty." This, too, is an idiom and not to be taken literally.

Illustration 3

1. Why do you think Rose dumped the water out of the bucket? *(Answers will vary; probably just to make the point that it wasn't fit to drink.)*

2. "Your poor sister's near dyin' for a drop of cool water" is another idiom, not to be taken literally.

Illustration 4

Vocabulary:

bramble bushes

1. Discuss "lit into me."

2. Discuss "word of honor."

Illustrations 5 & 6

Vocabulary:

peered

1. Discuss "tumbledown shack"—a dilapidated small cabin.

2. Can you see some chickens with only one leg and some with three or four? *(If you look hard, you can.)*

3. Did the cow moo? *(No, it sounded like a mule.)*

4. What sound did the chickens make? *(Whistled like mockingbirds.)*

Illustration 7

Vocabulary:

kindling   plaited   stone-mortar   pestle

1. What did the old woman put on her knees like a pumpkin? *(Her head.)*

2. What word do we usually use today instead of plait? *(Braid.)*

3. What do you think it means to "grind it in the stone mortar"? *(Answers will vary.)*

Illustration 8

1. Discuss "frock-tail coats" and "trail-train dresses" using the illustrations.

2. Name the dances the rabbits did. *(Square dance, Virginia reel, cakewalk.)* Have you heard of all of them? *(Answers will vary.)*

Lesson 4

Discussion of the story can be divided at this point.

Illustration 9

1. The old woman said, "I got a present for you." Discuss the fact that sometimes poor language is used in literature because that's the way people really talk.

2. We finally meet up with the talking eggs. Do you think you could have followed directions as well as Blanche did? *(Answers will vary.)*

Illustrations 10 & 11

1. There are two good examples of metaphors on this page:

    "a handsome carriage that grew in a wink" and
    "a pony that sprouted from the size of a cricket"

    These are the type of expressions that allow the reader to see in his "mind's eye" what the author is saying. What is the author saying in these two metaphors? *(Answers will vary.)*

Illustration 12

Vocabulary:

gawked   finery   contrary

1. What does "rode . . . home like a grand lady" mean? *(Answers will vary.)*

2. Discuss the attitude change in the mother.

3. Compare this page with the guesses made when discussing the illustrations.

Illustrations 13 & 14

Vocabulary:

dawdled

1. "Drag-foot" is probably a made-up word. Does it illustrate to the reader in words what Rose's attitude was? *(Answers will vary.)*

2. How did Rose react when she got near the old woman's cabin? *(She laughed.)*

3. What is Rose calling "stupid"? *(The sight of it all.)*

Illustration 15

1. Why did Rose have to go to bed hungry? *(She made fun of everything and wouldn't do what she was told to do.)*

2. After reading this page, does it help to better understand the illustration? *(Answers will vary.)*

3. Why do you think the illustrator made this picture from a rear view? *(Answers will vary, but note that both times the old woman removes her head, the reader does not really see her without a head.)*

Illustration 16

Vocabulary:

groping

1. Did you think all along that Rose would act the way she did? *(Answers will vary.)*

2. How could we describe what kind of a person Rose is? *(Greedy, stingy, etc.)*

Illustration 17

Vocabulary:

hightailed

1. Have you ever heard the expression: "hollering bloody murder"? *(Answers will vary.)*

2. What was chasing Rose? *(Snakes, toads, frogs, yellowjackets, wasps, and a big gray wolf.)*

Illustration 18

Vocabulary:

generous

1. Would you say this book had a happy ending? *(Probably.)*

2. What do you think happened to the old woman? *(Answers will vary.)*

CONCLUDING CRITICAL THINKING EXERCISES

1. *The Talking Eggs* is not a fable, but it does teach a lesson or moral. Think of one that would be appropriate and be able to defend why you thought of it.

2. Compare and contrast Blanche and Rose. Do you think it makes a difference that Rose was the older of the two?

3. Compare the illustrations of this book with those in *Lon Po Po*. In the Caldecott Awards for 1990, *Lon Po Po* won the award and *The Talking Eggs* was one of the honor books. Do you agree with this or not? Provide good reasons for your answer and be able to support it.

4. Use the general theme of this book and rewrite it for modern times.

5. Think of an action by Blanche and how you would have handled it differently. Explain why you would have handled it that way.

6. Imagine that you are Blanche. Tell how you felt when you went home with the water.

7. Write an extension to this book telling more about the old woman and/or Blanche.

8. Create an original character or animal and tell how it would fit into *The Talking Eggs*.

CONCLUDING EXTENSION ACTIVITIES

Suggestions for specific as well as general activities that can be used with this book follow. A complete list of general activities can be found at the end of the book.

1. Think of four opinion-type questions based on this book and survey your classmates (or anyone else who might have read *The Talking Eggs*). Make a graph of the results.

2. Draw a map of the area where *The Talking Eggs* takes place. You will want to include Rose and Blanche's house, the old woman's shack, the well, and the city.

3. Make finger puppets of the characters and act out the story.

4. Make a picture dictionary of some of the more colorful words in *The Talking Eggs*.

5. Write out the title decoratively and for each letter write something about *The Talking Eggs*.

6. With some of your friends, act out the story of *The Talking Eggs*.

7. Research crickets and try to find out why the expression "sharp as a cricket" would have come about.

8. Various kinds of music and dancing are associated with the American South. Demonstrate the Virginia reel and the cakewalk. You may have to research one or both of these.

9. Decorate some eggs, making them as pretty as possible. (The eggs should be hard-boiled or the insides should be blown out!)

OTHER BOOKS
BY ROBERT D. SAN SOUCI

The Legend of Scarface: A Blackfeet Indian Tale. Garden City, N.Y.: Doubleday, 1981.

Song of Sedna: Sea-Goddess of the North. Garden City, N.Y.: Doubleday, 1981.

Brave Little Tailor. Garden City, N.Y.: Doubleday, 1982.

Legend of Sleepy Hollow. Garden City, N.Y.: Doubleday, 1986.

Young Merlin. Garden City, N.Y.: Doubleday, 1990.

OTHER BOOKS ILLUSTRATED BY
JERRY PINKNEY

Arkhurst, Joyce Cooper. *The Adventures of Spider: West African Folk Tales.* Boston: Little Brown, 1964.

Hamilton, Virginia. *Time Ago: Tales of Jahdu.* N.Y.: Greenwillow, 1980.

Taylor, Mildred D. *Roll of Thunder, Hear My Cry.* (Newbery Medal) New York: Dial, 1976.

Bibliography

Bosma, Bette. *Fairy Tales, Fables, Legends and Myths: Using Folk Literature in Your Classroom.* New York: Teacher's College Press, 1987.

Carpenter, Humphrey & Prichard. *Oxford Companion to Children's Literature.* London: Oxford University Press, 1984.

Cummire, Ann (Ed.). *Something About the Author* (Vols. 1-55). Detroit: Gale Research, Inc., 1985.

de Regniers, Beatrice Schenk. *May I Bring A Friend?* Illustrated by Beni Montresor. New York: Atheneum, 1964.

Hodges, Margaret (Retold by). *Saint George and the Dragon.* Illustrated by Trina Schart Hyman. Boston: Little, Brown, 1984.

Lobel, Arnold. *Frog and Toad Are Friends.* New York: Harper and Row, 1970.

Lionni, Leo. *Alexander and the Wind-Up Mouse.* New York: Pantheon, 1969.

Marshall, James (Retold by). *Goldilocks and the Three Bears.* Illustrated by James Marshall. New York: Dial Books for Young Readers, 1988.

Ness, Evaline. *Sam, Bangs & Moonshine.* New York: Holt, Rinehart and Winston, Inc. 1966.

San Souci, Robert D. *The Talking Eggs.* Illustrated by Jerry Pinkney. New York: Dial Books for Young Readers. 1989.

Sauliner, Karen Luczak (Adaptor). *Goldilocks and the Three Bears in Signed English.* Illustrated by Ralph R. Miller. Washington D.C.: Gallaudet College Press.

Steig, William. *Sylvester and the Magic Pebble.* New York: Windmill Books, 1969.

Yorinks, Arthur. *Hey Al.* Illustrated by Richard Egielski. New York: Farrar, Straus, and Giroux, 1986.

Young, Ed. (Translated by). *Lon Po Po.* Illustrated by Ed Young. New York: Philomel Books, 1989.

Zelinsky, Paul O. (Retold by). *Rumpelstiltskin.* Illustrated by Paul Zelinsky. New York: E. P. Dutton, 1986.

Zemach, Harve (Retold by). *Duffy and the Devil.* Illustrated by Margot Zemach. New York: Farrar, Straus, and Giroux, 1973.

General Extension Activities

Most of the following extension activities can be modified and used with any literature book. Many of them have been used one way or another in this book as Concluding Activities. They are fun activities that can be used to tie up the study of a book.

1. Rewrite the story in the form of a play or puppet show.

2. Make puppets of the characters for a show by cutting them out of wallpaper and gluing them to the end of a straw.

3. Skim through the book and write as many color words as you can find. With your crayon, write the color of the word. You might want to put these in a booklet in the shape of a character in the story.

4. Fold a large piece of paper into eight sections. Draw a different part of the story in each section and then retell the story in your own words to another group who have not read or heard the story.

5. Make a cassette tape, reading the story so that other children can read along. You will want to use some kind of a noise to indicate when it's time to turn the page.

6. Reproduce the Story Mapping outline on large chart paper. If the children are advanced enough, give each a small copy to fill out at the same time.

7. Make a time line of the events in the life of one of the characters. Or develop a time line to keep track of the events as they happened in the story.

8. Make a chart or poster so that others will want to read this book. Make it as colorful as possible.

9. Design a bulletin board about this book. (A project for older children could be to use an opaque projector and reproduce the illustrations from the book.)

10. Make finger puppets of all the characters and then act out the story.

11. Design a new original book cover for the book.

12. Make one or more bookmarks for the book using the characters portrayed in the story.

13. Create an original character or animal and tell how it would fit into the story.

14. Make a diorama of one of the scenes of the story.

15. Make sentence strips of the story. Cut the strips apart and then see if someone in the group can regroup them in the correct sequential order.

16. Make a project cube of the story. Before folding it into a cube, draw six different scenes for the story.

17. Create a cartoon or comic book retelling the story.

18. Write new lyrics to a known tune and retell the story in song.

19. Conduct a survey of your classmates as to how they liked this book. Make a graph of your results.

20. Create a collage of words, pictures, and/or phrases about the book. Use magazines, colored paper, cloth or other materials for this.

21. Rewrite this book as a play or a puppet show.

22. Reproduce the Contrasting—Real and Not Real on large chart paper. (A small copy can be used by the students.) Go through each of the animal characters presented and fill out the chart together.

23. Make a "thumbprint" book about your book (the characters come from fingers dipped in paint or on an ink pad) and then write captions for these illustrations.

24. Make a "WANTED" poster for one of the characters.

25. Use any type of clay or play dough and make a sculpture of the characters in this book.

26. Retell the story from memory as a group. Write this story on the board.

27. Write out the title decoratively, in a vertical manner. For each letter, write a phrase about the book.

28. Draw a map of the area where the story takes place.

29. Make a picture dictionary of some of the nouns (naming words) in the book.

30. Compose three new titles for the story that would give the reader an idea what the story is about.

Story Map

When you are reading a story, it is sometimes easy to "map out" the story. Starting with the characters and the setting, list the problem and goal as you meet them in the book. The episodes can be jotted down as you come to them, including the beginning, the development, and the outcome of each episode. This will lead to the final resolution, or conclusion, of the story. Make a large "map" similar to the one below (or for the overhead) and fill it out as you read the book. The students might enjoy small copies.

Title _____

Characters: (Who) _____ **Setting:**

_____ (Where)_____

_____ (When) _____

_____ _____

_____ _____

_____ _____

Problem: (What) _____

_____

_____

Action: 1. _____

2. _____

3. _____

4. _____

5. _____

6. _____

Solution: _____

_____

Compare

When you want to compare one thing or character to another, use this form.

Attribute Listing

Attribute listing is listing the good things and the bad things about a character or an idea. Use this worksheet for your attribute listing.

Good	Bad

Contrast

After reading a book, use this form to contrast one thing or person with another.

Venn Diagram

When you want to compare or contrast one thing or character to another and there is some area of overlap, use this form.

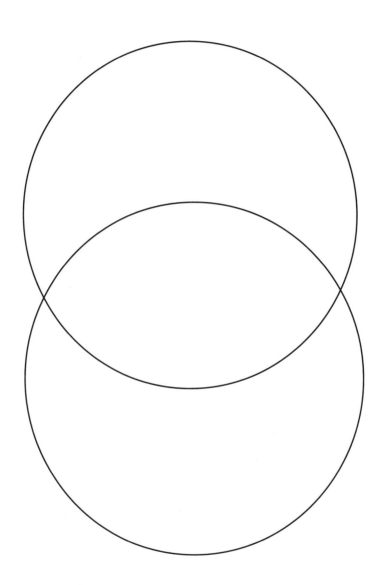

Character Webbing

Put the name of the book in the center rectangle. Then, as you meet new characters in the story, write down their names in a side rectangle and something about them. This can be just one word, or several. Don't try to do this all at once. Remember that you will probably meet each character again. Your opinion about the character may change as you get further in the story.

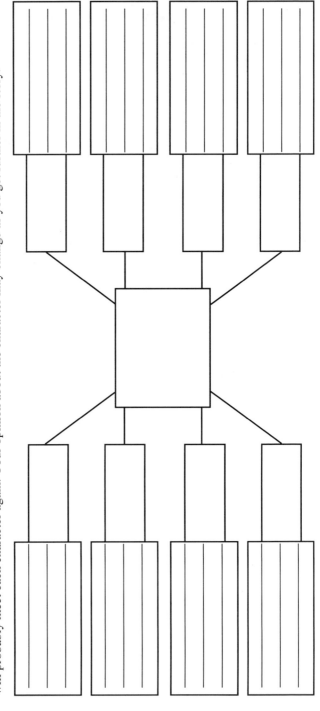